Freckles to Wrinkles

a Silver Boomer Book

Editors:
Ginny Greene
Becky Haigler
Kerin Riley-Bishop
Barbara B. Rollins

Silver Boomer Books
Abilene Texas

Some selections in Freckles to Wrinkles have been published previously.

"Afternoon at Grandfather's House" – *Artella web site* ~§~ "Guard Duty" – *Chicken Soup for the Horse Lover's Soul* ~§~ "The Gate" – *Streetlight* ~§~ "Nearing Menopause, I Run into Elvis at Shoprite" – *Karamu* (Word Press), *Grow Old Along with Me* (Papier-Mache Press) ~§~ "The Fifties" – *Rattle, Radiance* (Word Press) ~§~ "Creamed Spinach" – *Echolocation* ~§~ "Ballet Class" – *Coffee Break Poetry (www.cafepress.com)* ~§~ "Spring Fever" – *Imprint: Enlightening, thought-provoking and uplifting poetry* ~§~ "Expect Joy, Expect Blessings" – *www.boomerwomenspeak.com* (July 2007), excerpts *The Hip Grandma's Handbook* ~§~ "Gumming of Age" – another version published by *flashquake* ~§~ "Killing a Frog" – *Plum Ruby Review* (December 2003/January 2004), *Contemporary American Voices* (August 2007) ~§~ "Wild Sugar" – *Acorn* (Universities West Press Anthology) ~§~ "Red Tide" – small literary journal *Skyline Magazine* (June-August, 2007) ~§~ "Tip Boxes" – *Coe Review* (Vol. 37, No. 1, Fall 2006) ~§~ "Carol Lee Turns 60..." – *Erato* (February 25, 2005) ~§~ "Meet Frankenstein" – *poetrymagazine.com* and *Greatest Hits: 1975-2000*, James Penha (Pudding House) ~§~ "Four on a Fold" – *Brother* (Action Press, 1996), and *Boomer Girls: Poems by Women from the Baby Boom Generation* (University of Iowa Press) ~§~ An earlier version of "Education" – *When I Was a Child: A Poetic Collection of Childhood Impressions* (PoetWorks Press, 2003) ~§~ "Bridging a Woman's Life" *Houston Poetry Fest Anthology 2005* ~§~ "Bloodlines" – *Capper's Magazine* (October 2000) ~§~ "Expect Blessings; Expect Joy" *Boomer Women Speak web site* ~§~ "Connie Sue's Concerns" – *North of New Orleans* (Summer 2004) ~§~ "Graying in my Life" – *The Lost American: From Exile to Freedom*

FRECKLES TO WRINKLES. Copyright © 2008. Published by Silver Boomer
    Books, 2998 South 14th Street #101, Abilene TX 79605, USA
Poetry and prose © 2008 by the authors
Cover art © 2008 by Barbara B. Rollins and Kerin Riley-Bishop
Other art © Steve Cartwright and Barbara B. Rollins
Other matter © 2008 by the editors

www.SilverBoomerBooks.com ~§~ SilverBoomerBooks@gmail.com
ISBN: 978-0-9802120-1-3

Dedication

*This volume is dedicated
to every freckled day
of our past
and every wrinkle
in our time.*

Ginny Greene

Becky Haigler

Kerin Riley-Bishop

Barbara B. Rollins

The Silver Boomer Books

Silver Boomers

a collection of prose and poetry

by and about baby boomers

March, 2008

Freckles to Wrinkles

July, 2008

This Path

Fall, 2008

"It is never too late to have a happy childhood." Tom Robbins ~§~

Table of Contents

"Four be the things I'd have been better without: love, curiosity,

recaptured." Jean Baudrillard ~§~ "A graceful and honorable old age

There was this freckle, and it got bigger and bigger." Bill Cosby ~§~

"Childhood is a disease - a sickness that you grow out of." William

Golding ~§~ "Wrinkles are hereditary. Parents get them from their

From Freckles...

Barbara B. Rollins

children." Doris Day ~§~ "Age does not bring you wisdom, age brings

Soundtrack

Barbara B. Rollins

Mary had a little lamb
my name is Sam, Sam I am
hippity hop, hippity hop
here I come, ready or not

push 'em back, push 'em back
yackity yack, don't talk back
he loves me yes, he loves me not
he said he'd call, but he forgot

a hundred bottles of beer on the wall
yes, Mom, I know, I meant to call
grades are out, I got a C
next week we're playing Tennessee

here comes the bride
hand in hand and side by side
hush little baby, don't you cry
mommy's got to go now, kiss me 'bye

wash your hands and comb that hair
the hundredth time, we're almost there
don't jerk the wheel – slow – whoa
have you settled yet on where to go

this house just echoes it's so quiet
I'm playing bridge next Thursday night
don't forget the passports, Dear
I told you that! You just don't hear

grow old with me, the best is yet
Dad's laugh and hugs we won't forget
I shall wear purple, red hats, too
yes, Sweetie, Grams kiss your booboo

the thing that flies, yes, a plane
where did I put my walking cane
I didn't hear a thing she said
I don't hear much outside my head

I thought I'd teach the world to sing
but now I mess up everything
when words and names I know won't come
then in my head the whole earth hums

Riding Into Time

Lisa Timpf

He was brown, with a black mane and tail and white socks. If he had a name, I don't remember it.

I saw him whenever I accompanied my parents to the grocery store in town. Depositing a dime into the coin slot would bring him to life, this mechanical horse, and for a few handfuls of seconds, the lucky child for whom that ride had been purchased would sit on the saddle, feet firmly planted in the western-style stirrups, eyes closed to block out the store and the shoppers, the better to visualize the open range or some similar fantasy setting.

As a youngster, I didn't have a plentiful supply of coins of any description. And so my opportunity to taste the magic of the mechanical horse was at the whim of my father.

I knew better than to ask. My dad usually refused selfish requests. Non-verbal communication, however, was fair game. And so, I would slow down just a bit and give the horse a lingering look as we walked past – for the horse was strategically positioned in such a way that every outgoing shopper had no choice but to walk by him.

And sometimes Dad would ask, "Would you like a ride?" and I would scramble up on the horse's back, quick, before he could change his mind, and sit there, gripping the reins tightly, waiting for the horse to lunge to life.

And other times, the majority of times, we just walked past.

wrinkles on thy cheeks." Thomas Browne ~§~ "When you finally go

Now, I don't mean to sound as if my dad was cheap, or mean, for he was not. Though I was oblivious to it at the time, I realize now that by the time the bills were paid, my father didn't have a whole lot more disposable cash than I did. A few seconds' worth of riding on a mechanical horse provided no benefit beyond a soon-vanished pleasure, and would have seemed an immense extravagance, a waste of hard-earned money. And so I have some appreciation, now, of the inner struggle he must have experienced as he looked at my face, and the horse, as we headed out of the store with a cartload of carefully selected groceries.

My father died a few years back, and the mechanical horse and his cousins are long gone from the grocery stores in our parts. Yet I can clearly remember those few treasured rides – made the more pleasurable by the times we walked past. For my father may have known this as well: a thing is sometimes made more precious not because we do it all the time, but because we do not.

Four on a Fold

Paula Sergi

Some summer nights in the early sixties
in the middle of the country,
no ocean for thousands of miles
in either direction,
the air was everywhere heavy
like grandma's mothballed wool quilt,

---

back to your old hometown, you find it wasn't the old home you missed

navy as night
covering our faces, holding us down.
We should've been tired from play —
four square, seven steps around the house,
hopscotch drawn from the sharp side of a stone
on squares of concrete that marked
the edge of our front lawn.
Those nights we could stay up till nine,
but even after sunset no air moved.
We'd try to sleep
in the ten-by-twelve family room,
windows on three sides,
as if the screens themselves
would make a breeze.
Four on a fold-down couch
in short polyester pajamas
that stuck to our backs
waiting for sleep,
for a breeze, for a father
who never came back to say good-bye.
I worried maybe we'd all suffocate
before dawn, but we all grew up
one way or another
before we realized
how little air we'd had.

Charley Plays a Tune
Michael Lee Johnson

Crippled with arthritis
in a dark rented room
Charley plays
melancholic melodie
on a dust-filled
harmonica he
found abandoned
on a playground of sand
years ago by a handful of children
playing on monkey bars.
He now goes to the bathroom on occasion,
peeing takes forever; he feeds the cat,
Melody, when he buys fish at the local market
and the skeleton bones of the fish show through.
He lies on his back riddled with pain,
pine cones fill his pillows and mattress;
praying to Jesus and rubbing his rosary beads
Charley blows tunes out his
celestial instrument
notes float through the open window
touch the nose of summer clouds.
Charley overtakes himself with grief
and is ecstatically alone.
Charley plays a solo tune.

Unbreakable
Juleigh Howard-Hobson

It is 1969. I am six. I am in my grandmother's kitchen. My grandmother loves beautiful things. She has them everywhere, but especially here, in her favorite room in her house.

Her pots have colors on the outside. She has a pink one, a green one, a great big orange one. One pot is white, bright white, with a line of red on the rim of it and on the handle, too. Her mixing bowls make a rainbow when you line them up.

She has fancy dishes up in the cupboard but her everyday dishes are more wonderful. They are Melmac – real Melmac – and she has green, yellow, red, blue, pink, and fleck grey. Some are the color of the inside of a cantaloupe. When you put the different colored ones all on top of each other, cup, bowl, sandwich dish, supper dish, they look like candy towers.

She says when she dies she will leave all of them to me in her will.

My mother says good, I don't want them that's for sure.

I smile.

I sip strawberry milk from a lime green cup that I put on a butter yellow saucer. My tuna-fish sandwich, cut in four squares, is on a plate that is the same color of the sky. These are my favorites.

Carefully I replace the cup to the saucer when I am done. Carefully I pile them up, cup and saucer, like Necco wafers, on the blue dish. Carefully I carry them to the sink.

childhood dies, its corpses are called adults." Brian W. Aldiss ~§~

Even though they are my grandmother's Melmac dishes,
now they are mine, too.
My grandmother smiles as we wash them, together.

Ballet in the Piney Woods
Glenda Beall

Little girl sunsuits littered the wiregrass.
Summer warmed small bronze bodies
that danced on the stage of a fallen oak,
to songbirds' music from the mayhaw.

They felt, at five, the kiss of butterflies
upon their eyes, breathed honeysuckle air.
Like sylphs set free they twirled, arms open,
gathering the breeze against their bareness.

Chastised for their boldness by older girls
who barged into their glade,
the innocents saw themselves
and were ashamed.

"Wear a smile and have friends; wear a scowl and have wrinkles."

Ramblings of a Long Since Ex-Paper Boy

Larry Lefkowitz

Some decades have passed since I was a paper boy. Or a boy who delivered papers, as a "paper boy" seemed to put me in the same class as paper airplanes and paper boats. Of the latter two categories, paper airplanes would have been closer to the mark. For I would throw the papers from my bicycle in the hoped-for direction of the front door in hoped-for emulation of a plane coming in for a landing. Unfortunately, my mastery of aerodynamics was not good. The paper usually planed off or veered off or flew off in other directions, landing on – or even in – hedges, gardens, various other sites which would have made nice places to read them. But my customers, for some reason, preferred to receive their papers on their front door stoops.

Perhaps they would have been mollified if the papers arriving at various points on their frontal property had remained crisply folded. If I was a poor thrower, I was a worse folder. The papers often flew open in mid-flight, which made a pretty sight to me but a disturbing one to my customers. They apparently preferred to open the paper themselves instead of having it already opened for them. Or perhaps they rued having to reconstruct the paper so that each page followed the previous in numbered order. It would have been far easier to read

George Eliot ~§~ "I don't want my wrinkles taken away – I don't want

whatever page ended up first, but try to teach an old reader new tricks....

If memory serves me right, the favored paper fold in those days was not the simple folding in of the sides to make a cylinder, but a more complicated folding into a square. I did not excel at this fold. It was a fold designed for controlled flight. In my case, the paper flew more in the manner of a kite than a missile.

Still, my customers stayed with me. Pity on their part, or personality on my part, or maybe something I touched within them, manifesting the less than perfect in life, struck a chord.

Surely, in the not far future, electronic delivery to a screen will make the paper boy obsolete. The sight and sound of a paper flying through the air and landing with a pleasant whack will disappear from American life. The feel of a newspaper, the odor of a newspaper, will go also. Progress, they will call it. If I'm still around, I won't.

1 Find

TJ Coles

I find that I, as time goes by,
Sometimes forget the what and the why.
I sit by myself doing whatever I do.
Reading a book or polishing a shoe.

When suddenly something jumps in my mind.
I must go, I must run, I must seek and then find.

I rise from my place and proceed with due haste,
Certain of my duty and sure of my pace.

I arrive when I get there all ready to go.
But whatever I came for, I no longer know.
The impulse is there, there was something I sought.
But now, it seems I can't remember just what.

There is something I need. I'm sure of it now.
It'll come back to me, someway or somehow.
I wait and I pace like a cat in a cage.
The answer won't come, the mind won't engage.

I finally give up and go back to my shoe.
Who knows what I thought I wanted to do.
It's only when the chair finally hits my behind
That I remember once more what I wanted to find.

I jump up again and go back where I looked
Only to find that once more I've been rooked.
What ever it was that I wanted to find
Must somehow connect with my chair and behind.

It's my memory you see, it comes and it goes.
Sometimes it ebbs and sometimes it flows.
There's no point in throwing a hissy fit.
It only comes back in my chair, when I sit.

I think if just maybe I wrote it all down
It might just stay long enough to be found.
So I'll just go get some paper and pen…
Now tell me, what was I here for again?

---

man, As morning shows the day." John Milton ~§~ *"If wrinkles must*

The Fifties

Barbara Crooker

We spent those stifling, endless, summer afternoons
on hot front porches, cutting paper dolls from Sears
catalogs, making up our own ideal families
complete with large appliances
and an all-occasion wardrobe with fold-down
paper tabs.
Sometimes we left crayons on the cement
landing, just to watch thcm mclt.
We followed the shade around the house.
Time was a jarful of pennies, too hot
to spend, stretching long and sticky,
a brick of Bonomo's Turkish Taffy.
Tomorrow'd be more of the same,
ending with softball or kickball,
then hide-and-seek in the mosquitoey dark.
Fireflies, like connect-the-dots or find-the-hidden-
words, rose and glowed, winked on and off,
their cool fires coded signals
of longing and love
that we would one day
learn to speak.

be written upon our brows, let them not be written upon the heart.

Mud Puddle Frolics
Betty Jo Goddard

It was May and school was still in session when the weather turned hot. Graciously, it chose Friday night for a storm. Dark, looming clouds rolled in from the west, thunder boomed, lightning crackled, and wind raged. Rain pelted our roof, filling our rain barrel in no time and dripping through our ceiling into the waiting pots below.

If Windsor's streets had storm gutters, there were none near our house. Water filled ditches and lapped across the road. As soon as we kids got up, we looked through mom's lace curtains and saw water lapping across Virginia Avenue. We bolted down our oatmeal and started in on Mom.

"Mom, can we go out wading?"

She raised her eyebrows. "Can? I think you're all able to wade, but you don't have permission to."

"May," we chorused. "May. May we at least go barefoot?"

You'd think, with all this bleating, that going barefoot was the greatest thing in the world, but I didn't really like going barefoot all that much. The rocks hurt my feet, I couldn't run as fast, and I didn't like getting my feet dirty. Despite this, that huge puddle drew me like a bee to honey.

"Can we? May we? May we, please, pretty please?"

Possibly to relieve her ears, Mom caved in. "Oh, all right, then. But you be sure to wash your feet when you come in. I'll put a bucket by the rain barrel."

The spirit should never grow old." James A. Garfield ~§~ "I like the

We kids shucked off our shoes and headed for that mud puddle, slamming the screen door behind us. Muddy water rose over my ankles and up my legs. Delicious. I pushed my shins against the water, swirling it in waves up to my knees, enjoying cool streams rolling down my calf. A fly landed on my arm, tickling it. I brushed it away with a watery hand as I churned toward Jim.

Just as I came alongside him, Jim stomped. Water splashed over my thighs, wetting the hem of my dress.

"Oh, ho. Too bad for you, Jim!" Bent on retaliation, I clenched my teeth, stuck out my chin, and, with determined vigor, matched Jim stomp for stomp. Then I turned and churned through the water away from my foe. At the end of the puddle, I eyed Jim as he headed toward me, his pant legs rolled up above his knees. Not to be cowed, I waded toward the center of the pool. Jim feinted, then stomped hard, sending a giant spray over my front. I circled to Jim's left side where the water was deepest and thrust my foot down. A gratifying geyser of muddy water splashed clear up to Jim's face. Laughing, I waded off with Jim plunging after me.

"All right for you," Jim said. When he reached me, he jumped high and landed with both feet, dousing me. Water dripped from my chin, from my nose, from my eyebrows. This was war.

Jim and I stomped in earnest. Splashes flew. We lurched backwards, arms reeling from "accidental" shoves. Jim's rolled up pants legs were drenched; my fresh print dress dripped.

Mary Lena, our little sister, liked the splashing game. Heedless of her sun suit, she stooped down, cupped her hands, and threw water to the skies. Laughing, John mimicked Jim and me. Stamping his chubby legs, he happily splattered. Tom, who barely knew how to walk, toddled toward the water and sat right down in it. It wasn't long before all of us had a lot more than our feet wet.

Since our clothes were already wet, why couldn't we? Leaving Tom behind, Jim, John, Mary Lena, and I dashed inside and petitioned Mom. "See, we on accident got a little bit wet, so please, can we sit down in the water and get all the way wet? Please, pretty please, can we? May we?"

Mom suffered our shrill pleas while she surveyed our spattered clothes. Assent was the path of least resistance. Exasperated, she said, "Oh, all right. Go ahead."

Banging the screen door, we thundered out and headed for the mud puddles. Now real splashing began. With great arm thrusts, Jim and I splashed each other, showering water in a veritable deluge. Reveling in the sensuous feeling of getting wet all over, I jumped up and landed, splat, on my seat, showering Jim with a giant spray of water and mud. Going barefoot wasn't half bad when we could do this.

After we had our fill of puddle splashing, Mom took her washtub to the back yard and, bucketful after bucketful, filled it with water from the rain barrel. "Now you kids get in there and rinse all the mud off before you come into the house. Every bit of it. Betty Jo, you help the little ones. Get the mud out of their hair, too."

So, as the May sun beat hot on our shoulders and rainwater splashed cool on our arms, we kids enjoyed more frolicking in our backyard washtub pool. Altogether, the morning was wonderful fun, and we were out of Mom's hair for an hour or two. Back in the 1930's, none of us – not even Mom and Dad – had dreamed of television or computer games. But we didn't need that stuff, even if we'd known about it. A good night's rainstorm provided us with a whole Saturday morning of rowdy entertainment.

Bloodlines

Becky Haigler

Three figures stand against a soddy
in the Oklahoma dustbowl, as if awaiting
execution or reprieve. In the foreground
Henry Ford's machine is clearly
the occasion for the picture.

"Uncle Brad's Model A," said a grown-up.
I didn't care for the car. I stared at the woman:
tall and bony, sad eyes in wire-rimmed glasses,
mouth drooping under a long nose,
hair not captured by the shapeless hat.

"Uncle Brad, Aunt Emma and Grandma."
"...the soddy Grandma lived in
when she came to Indian Territory."
"Emma never was a pretty girl."
Comments followed the picture 'round the table.

"It's me!" I claimed what others were too polite to say,
but I knew. Two generations and a side-step ago —
my father's father's sister had my face. No matter
that she was ugly, that we were ugly. Instead,
a sense of belonging, being connected, to Emma's face.

A Cowboy and His Horse

TJ Coles

Horses were very important to me when I was a kid, because of my decision to become a cowboy. It's a well-known fact that any cowboy worthy of the name has to have a horse. This was difficult because we lived in the city most of the time. The only time I had a chance to ride was when we were visiting my Grandmother's ranch. Even then, the only horse I was allowed to ride was Snowfire.

Don't let the name fool you. Snowfire had a white coat, that's where the snow part of her name came from. Her fire however had long since gone out. She was very nearly as wide as she was long. She was so big that when I sat on her I was almost doing the splits. Two small kids riding bareback could sit side by side without fear of falling off. She was mild mannered and gentle – you could put a little one up on her back and have no fear that she would buck him off no matter what he did. She was also so slow you could leave the child on her for an hour and they would both still be within sight of the house.

Snowfire and I spent many wonderful hours together. I would be riding along staring meaningfully at the horizon on my way to save the ranch from the Indians or rustlers or flood, fire, disaster or whatever. Snowfire would be meandering along nibbling on anything that looked interesting along the way. If things got too boring, I could just stretch out on her back and take a nap.

that I'm older. I like it – despite the wrinkles. It's what I feel inside

Those were good times, but perhaps not as exciting as they might have been. One day I decided it was time for a real adventure. I'd ride over the mountain and down to Piney Creek. There could be rustlers or stampeding cattle along the way; even if there weren't, at least I'd be out of sight of the house.

I would take my BB gun along for protection and maybe shoot a grouse for the supper pot. I had never actually shot a grouse but I was ever hopeful. The trip was a little over two miles. Taking into account Snowfire's best pace, I figured it would take us all day, so I packed a lunch.

Because this was an adventure, I put a saddle and bridle on Snowfire. Once everything was lashed down or otherwise securely tied, I grabbed the reins and swung into the saddle and we lit a shuck out of there swinging high and wide. That is to say, by hammering my heels repeatedly into her sides I managed to get Snowfire up to the blistering pace of may be three or four miles per hour and headed more or less in the right direction.

The next hours were pure high adventure hampered only by Snowfire's propensity for sampling every stray outcropping of vegetation that she came across, making our actual progress approximately that of an anemic snail. We finally reached the top of the pass about noon. Because we were making such good time, I decided to eat lunch in the saddle. Snowfire didn't need a break to eat because she had been eating more or less continuously since we started.

We finally made it to Piney Creek about six in the evening and stopped just long enough for Snowfire to drink her fill, then turned around and headed back. Based on our progress up to that point, I figured we'd get back to the house in time for breakfast. But once she realized that we were headed back toward the barn, her whole attitude changed. It was like riding on a new horse.

Her walk was no longer a slow meander from one grassy bunch to the next. At one point she even broke into a trot. Soon we were walking along briskly, Snowfire no doubt picturing a warm stall and perhaps a scoop or two of oats, when there was a rustle of brush at the side of the road ahead of us. Snowfire snorted and clamped on the brakes. She came to a sudden and complete stop. She was an old cutting horse and could stop on a dime. Her rider, however, was not nearly as competent and was certainly not ready to stop.

I was thrown forward over the saddle onto her neck; on the way I happened to catch some of the more delicate portions of my body on the saddle horn. I was in a precarious position. I had both my arms and legs wrapped around Snowfire's neck. She did a very quick twisting and spinning motion, which dislodged me from her neck. She left me sitting in the middle of the road, clutching my injuries and watching her blaze back down the road, stirrups flapping and tail held high. I sat there wondering what in the heck had gotten into that dang horse. Who would have thought that fat horse could move so fast?

I was sitting there in the road thinking bad thoughts about my trusty steed when a movement caught my eye. I turned my head and, standing right there in the road, a little ways away, was a full-grown mountain lion. Well, full-grown might be an exaggeration. On sober reflection, looking back over thirty-some-odd years, I'm quite sure that this was a yearling cat probably no more than three quarters grown, but from the perspective of that ten-year-old sitting on the road, this was one really big kitty.

I was sitting with my knees up, hands cradling my bruised parts, and staring at a mountain lion, who was staring back from a distance, which I am here to tell you, was not nearly far enough away. I had absolutely no faith that my BB gun would be of any use in this situation, but I really wished that I had it in my hands instead of strapped to Snowfire's saddle. Maybe I could use it as a club.

The big cat was watching me closely, mentally picking out the parts of me it wanted to eat first. I started to get to my feet, getting ready to begin running as fast as I could in the direction Snowfire had gone. The cat crouched as if in preparation to spring at me so I sat back and started talking.

"Nice kitty, good kitty, you're such a pretty kitty." I was babbling, I knew it, but I couldn't help myself.

"You're such a good kitty. You wouldn't want to eat me, kitty. I wouldn't taste good. If I ever catch up with that dang horse I'm going to pull all her tail hairs out!"

The mountain lion relaxed a little, his ears came up and he looked puzzled. He hadn't expected to have a conversation with his dinner, who also happened to be a blathering idiot.

I continued to babble. The big cat finally sat up and looked around with an anxious expression. I watched while words continued to pour out of my mouth. Perhaps he was afraid one of his friends might see us together. That made me laugh out loud. When that peal of laughter came out, the lion jumped back several feet and began to cock his head one side to the other. I dissolved into a fit of giggles undoubtedly brought on by stress. I couldn't stop. Finally, I fell over on my side giggling, tears running down my face. Somewhere, my rational mind was thinking, "This is great. A cougar eats me because I'm laughing so hard I can't defend myself."

The cougar finally turned and trotted off into the woods, no doubt thinking that I was a raving lunatic and probably diseased. Moments later, I managed to get hold of myself and took off running down the road in the profound hope the mountain lion wouldn't change his mind. I headed to the main ranch. Snowfire had gone the other way. The heck with her. She left me on my

passage of life. They are what we have been through and who we want

own to face the cougar, so she could just take her chances. Besides, I seriously needed a change in underwear.

The journey up to the mountain had taken more than half a day. The way back took less than twenty minutes. I burst into the main house and blurted out my story to my grandfather. He dutifully listened, nodded his head, and commented that he hadn't seen a cougar in the neighborhood for more than ten years. But in the morning, we'd take the truck back up and see if we could spot it. I strongly suspected that he was taking my story less than seriously. So, I pointed out that his favorite horse was still up there with the mountain lion.

"Old Snowfire is smarter than any cougar she's likely to meet. Don't worry about her," he said.

But I did worry. Even though she had left me to face the cougar alone, she was still my trusty steed. Well maybe not so trusty. We had many hours together doing mostly whatever she wanted to do, but even so, I didn't want her to end up as lion food. I walked sadly down to the barn. I knew the cougar would get her. She was just too fat and too slow to get away.

There she was in her old stall. The saddle was hanging on the rack and her nose was in the feed trough sucking up oats. No wonder Granddad wasn't worried about her. She had beaten me home with enough time left over for him to unsaddle and feed her. She looked up at me and snorted in recognition, probably surprised that I had managed to get away from the lion.

"Yes, I got away, no thanks to you," I told her.

She snorted again and nuzzled me with her velvety nose. Anyone else might have thought that she was glad to see me or that she was apologizing for leaving me there on my own, but I knew her better than that. She was just hoping I would give her another scoop of oats.

---

to be." Lauren Hutton ~§~ "If God had to give a woman wrinkles, He

Killing A Frog

James Keane

Killing a frog
is easier than you think,
especially a baby one that can't hop
and doesn't blink,

picking gently among the wetted rocks

not to swim
to drink, perhaps to play
within the confines of a shallow brook,
green
with curiosity but nothing like fear
today.

A stone thrown here,
a stone thrown there
and still the baby one doesn't jump,
doesn't scare, though he does
stare ahead *(in growing dread?)* until

finally a direct hit shatters his head.

No scaring needed now,
no caring no how, just
staring into emptiness as
the baby one dies,
is dead.

---

might at least have put them on the soles of her feet." Ninon de

Another hit, and now his baby brain
lies, a pale green wafer, on the stone terrain.

I was there. I wanted to be.
I was not the only one.

But all I did was watch the killing done, though
I may have thrown a tiny little pebble, just one.

But I know I never hit him, I didn't, I swear
(as if anything killed would care).

If anyone older had happened upon us then,
they wouldn't have approved, but they wouldn't
have made a fuss; or maybe, to sound
serious, just a bit of
grown-up noise.

For, after all,
we were only
being boys.

The thing is,
of distance, age and time,
none for long has been my friend, none
has passed over the memory of this crime
to away and gone
to a merciful end. Never

ever for the unwitting stranger
to mercy, to danger,
to courage,
to caring, who couldn't stop
a simple horror, but won't

stop staring

L'Encolos ~§~ *"I'm shorter, I don't have as many freckles as Ron, and*

at the baby one
trying no longer to be a frog,
dying
at the unfeeling fingers of
growing children, though

graced with the empty love
of Almighty God, from Whom
all blessings, brooks

and dead frogs flow.

Ballet Class

Margaret Fieland

We walked down the dark street
to the Horn and Hardardt on Broadway
using our quarters to select
slices of pie
arrayed behind glass doors,

wondering whether June was getting too thin
or if we were getting too fat,

clattering down the subway stairs
to wait together for the train home.

And yet
I have lost the image of your face
and the sound of your name.

On the Road
Kathie Sutherland

When I was a child growing up in the 1950s and 1960s, my family spent many summers on the highway, enroute from one military base to another. Stuffed in a car or station wagon, favorite books, crayons and card games tucked into our suitcases, we'd read, sleep and argue our way across the country pausing to picnic, camp out and occasionally stay at a motel. From Edmonton to Montreal; Ontario to New Brunswick and then back over the Canadian Shield to the black dirt of the Manitoba prairie, and finally over the Rockies to Victoria at land's end we were always on the move.

There in the backseat I connected with my country, pleased that I could see what I'd learned from my geography books though the panorama of a side window. We visited museums and pored over route maps and in the quiet I dreamed that I was following in the footsteps of the Jesuit Fathers; paddling a canoe with French voyageurs; searching for buffalo with Native women on the Saskatchewan prairie; riding hard with Mounties as we chased down horse thieves. I even herded cattle with Alberta cowboys and drove a commemorative spike into the CPR (Canadian Pacific Railroad).

Even now when I'm on an airplane, aboard a Greyhound bus or even during a short trip on city transit, I return to this state of suspension and am released from my everyday concerns. When my husband suggested an overnight trip to the town of Rocky

---

wrinkles the soul." Douglas MacArthur ~§~ "Age imprints more

Mountain House recently, I leapt at the chance to enjoy the Alberta landscape. Settling into a comfortable silence, me in the passenger seat with a notebook on my lap and pen in hand, we headed west on Highway 39.

The canola fields were a sunshine yellow. Clumps of daisies were growing furiously by the roadside and barn swallows danced around old sheds, pleased to be nesting in the sagging roofs and collapsing walls. As the country sped by I caught sight of some cows grazing in thin shade of scrawny poplar trees, sleepy from the heat, oblivious to the tanker trucks and RVs rushing by. I thought about the people who once lived in these old homesteads, of men wiping the sweat from their faces as they picked rocks in the sun, women baking bread and hanging laundry where it was likely to catch a constant prairie wind.

As we traveled further west, I saw a white-tailed deer meandering along the edge of the forest, and later a coyote trotting across the ditch. An osprey circled above a wetland and fuchsia fireweed made an appearance in the long green grass and then orange lily-of-the-valley in the lowlands. As the red willow and cattails gave way to aspen and spruce, I searched the bogs and creeks for a glimpse of a moose.

Just outside Rocky Mountain House, a proliferation of signs announced the weekend's activities: a ball tournament, a horse show and "Bastion Days" at the Heritage Site. We were lucky to find a bed at Fox Ridge Bed & Breakfast. Our hosts gladly shared their knowledge of local attractions.

In the morning, after a restful night and congenial breakfast with a couple visiting from Yorkshire, England, we drove to the Heritage Site to learn about traditional Metis hunting techniques, watch demonstrations of long-barrel rifle handling, and storytelling by knowledgeable volunteers in period costumes. We drank Labrador tea and enjoyed hearing tales of rival fur trading companies told by an actor who tugged his wool

wrinkles in the mind than it does on the face." Michel de Montaigne

vest down over his belly and hitched up his plaid trousers, while telling us about other Scottish adventurers who ate from fine china hauled overland.

At the site of the original fort, where there is little left except depressions in the earth, I sat quietly listening to the wind and birds, and imagined the bustle of business as it might have been. I could almost hear horses snorting and leather saddles creaking, smell wood smoke and sweaty bodies, catch the sound of shouting as bateaux came into view around the bend in the North Saskatchewan River.

Satisfied with a large helping of Canadian history, we left the site and headed for home. Slipping back in time like this seems to put things in perspective for me. Both as a child learning Canadian history and as a woman searching for her own roots in story, the interior of a moving vehicle is an ideal space for resting in the flow of time and space.

My Next Ex-Wife
Quanah Parker

Met my first up in Oklahoma
 when I was just sweet sixteen.
I was a barback in a honky tonk
 where she kept the dishes clean.
Daddy was a preacher and he came in handy
 when we took our vows for life,
And she was, my friends, my first ex-wife.

~§~ *"Please don't retouch my wrinkles. It took me so long to earn*

My first ex-wife – how cruel can one girl be,
    to take a chance, make romance then a perfect fool of me.
My first ex-wife, I loved her heart and soul
    she was my one and only love until she had to go.

But she'd moved in with a Bible salesman
    when I came home from the war,
So I got hitched to a Wichita Widow,
    had legs clear out the door.
Next was a teacher from Texarkana;
    all she taught me was strife,
And she was, my friends, my last ex-wife.

Hold your hats and look what's comin'
    across that hardwood floor,
Long blond hair, ten years younger
    with legs clear out the door.
Pardon me boys, but moments like this
    only happen once in a life.
I think I just met...my next ex-wife.

My next ex-wife, oh who will that girl be?
    to have a chance to make romance then a perfect fool of me.
My next ex-wife, I'll love her heart and soul
    and probably I always will – till one of us must go.

Snow Ride

Denton Loving

The boy dressed to go out and sled for his first time. He was four, and this was the best snow of the winter so far, the first good snow of his young life.

Overnight, the winter storm had dumped half a foot of pure white powder. It looked like a sheet of butter-cream frosting spread on the world around the apartment complex. The parking lots, the sidewalks and yards, and the playground behind the buildings were covered.

His mother dressed him as warmly as an Eskimo child but in brighter colors. He wore a new red coat with a thick collar that buttoned around his neck, mittens and a wool toboggan she pulled down to cover his ears. His blue Spiderman galoshes were a size too big, meant to last for two winters. He was unsteady but getting used to walking in them.

This new world was so untouched and beautiful, he didn't want to disturb it. So he took longer strides in order to step in the existing foot prints. His mother watched from the corner of the building until he drew close to the other children.

It was still early, but already the back of the playground was full of neighborhood kids, also wrapped in boldly-colored winter clothes. They toted plastic sleds and garbage can lids with them, anything to carry their padded bodies down the slope behind the apartment buildings.

---

whereas a grown-up never wears out his short pants." Karl Kraus ~§~

At the bottom of the hillside ran Plum Creek, a shallow stream where he and his mother sometimes threw bread crumbs to the wild but friendly ducks. His mother had told him Plum Creek was likely frozen over. He couldn't imagine how this could be possible.

Like spiders dancing on a shared tapestry, one sled would skim downward, and somewhere nearby, another would follow. Up the steep hill, a child struggled back through the snow, dragging the sled, already eager for the thrill of the next ride down. Their movements became intricate designs left by ghost children and impossible to trace from beginning to end.

The boy rode down with the other children, ones he knew and trusted, who held his small body close to their own as they were pulled down the bank side. Now, though, he insisted on going alone, his solo sledding journey. An older girl, who sometimes babysat him, put him on a sled by himself, and when he was ready, she gave him a hearty push. Down he went, gliding in the wake of past sled marks, faster and faster down the hill, the air whipping his face.

It was the first time he felt the mystery of how a few seconds can speed by so quickly yet seem timeless, like a memory played in slow motion. He had no name for the sensation, but he wanted it never to end. It was the most freeing experience of the boy's life, and he soaked it in as the sled and his light body floated over the powdery white surface covering the earth. He relished every bounce and bump in the snow.

He reached the little flat place before the creek's bank, but the boy and the sled did not stop. He didn't want it to stop, and perhaps no one had told him how to stop anyway, to push his feet into the snow until they reached the hidden earth and slowed the sled. Plum Creek was in view now, and at this speed, he thought he would just keep going – over the creek bank, far past the other side, maybe never stopping again.

"When you're 50 you start thinking about things you haven't thought

But the sled did stop.

He was wet and cold when he realized he and the sled were in the slow, icy water of Plum Creek. It wasn't frozen over at all.

He stood in the creek and reached for the sled before climbing out. Water filled the extra space in his Spiderman boots. Up the hill, he trudged with the sled dragging behind him.

Cheers rang from the top of the hill. The older children welcomed him back with cries of congratulations and a few jokes. Their round breaths sent up smoke signals in the icy air. The others had mastered the descent, but none could remember such an exciting first flight.

Water still sloshed in his boots by the time he was taken home and dunked in a warm bath. His mother hovered over him. He was likely to catch pneumonia, his mother told him. She wrapped him in blankets and fed him chicken corn soup.

But the boy only worried the snow would melt before he could go out again. The thrill of the ride down hill – that one amazing moment – was worth everything else.

Veranda

Joy Harold Helsing

tired old man
in a wicker chair

tired old dog
on his own worn rug

just passing time

---

about before." Eugene O'Neill ~§~ "Even a minor event in the life of

The Mirror

Barbara Darnall

Why does my
grandmother's face
look back at me?
I didn't even like
the old woman much:
authoritative,
bitter,
stern.
Oh God,
don't let me
sound like her, too!

Why couldn't I
look more like
my mother's mother?
A gnarled stick,
but independent,
strong,
and kind,
who lived to be
eighty-three,
and then quietly
lost her mind.

a child is an event of that child's world and thus a world event." Gaston

Rituals

Mary Deal

Now that I'm single and dating again after nearly forty years of marriage, I'm finding I have a lot to catch up on.

"Jeffrey's not all there," my friends had warned.

As he and I became friends, I saw strange behaviors but nothing too unusual. At dinner, for instance, he would first eat all his mashed potatoes, then the bread, and then all his vegetables, followed by the meat. He never mixed foods and finished one before tackling another.

"Why not combine tastes?" I asked.

"Guess I can't break old habits," he said.

After seeing him do this time and time again, it began to bother me a little. He would finish one item, then pick up his plate and turn it so the next was in front of him. It seemed as if he ate all the other foods first, in order to sneak up on the meat.

One evening after dinner when he put on his jacket, he stretched his neck like a goose, like the neckline might be too tight. But the collar was open and in no way binding. These were strange behaviors, but not that weird. We all have rituals. I hoped my friends' warnings hadn't made me overly critical, but as time passed, I noticed other severe behaviors.

Every time we approached a crosswalk, he'd ceremoniously whack his fist four times against the black and white plaque that said "Push Button to Cross." Then he'd push the button. After seeing him do this a few times, I must have looked doubtful.

Bachelard ~§~ *"It takes three to make a child."* e. e. cummings ~§~ *"I*

"Hit the sign four times," he said. "The light will change in ten seconds."

"That's absurd," I said. "It's just a sign."

"A repairman told me that when I asked how to make the light change faster."

He believed the repairman who teased and played into his impatience? Not only was his behavior strange but so, too, was the belief in it.

People in cars at stoplights seemed puzzled when they watched him animatedly bang his fist, and I was embarrassed by their looks.

As weeks passed, I began to realize how deep his neuroses ran as I watched him for the umpteenth time stick a finger into his fly to make sure his zipper was up. Guys always do that. I do that, too, when I wear slacks, but not every few seconds!

That last time I saw him, we happened upon a crosswalk button where the instruction plaque and screws were missing. Clearly nothing was housed behind any plaque to affect the light changing. It was just an instructional sign. Everyone knew that, even the repairman.

The button below the missing plaque was not damaged and still clearly usable. "Quick, hit something, Jeffrey," I said, teasing. "We have to get across the street."

He goose-necked again and stared at the empty rectangular frame attached to the solid metal light pole. Finally, dead serious, he fingered his zipper and turned and walked away. "It's broken," he said, calling out over his shoulder. "Let's find another place to cross."

I pushed the button and the light changed. At that moment, I knew which direction I was headed. I also knew I would not be spending much time in the future with any guy who ate all his mashed potatoes first.

---

used to think getting old was about vanity – but actually it's about

Henhouse Treasures

Becky Haigler

I hold Nanny's hand when we uncover
the feed barrel. Sometimes rats hide there.
We scoop kernels of maize in a lard bucket
which serves to carry feed to the chickens
and eggs to the house.

In the chicken yard, Rhode Island reds
and leghorns, a ragged black rooster, peck
at imagined morsels and stray insects.
We empty our bucket by handfuls
to their cheerful greed.

We stoop to enter the chicken coop; smell
of old straw and feathers fills the dark.
Nearly every nest holds an oval offering
to be placed carefully in our bucket,
carried home and washed.

One old hen sits stubbornly. I am afraid to reach
past the pointed beak, under her warm featheredness.
"Gone broody," Nanny says, pushing the setting bird aside.
I carry the bucket of brown jewels,
accessory to the crime.

Death, Imperfect
Rhoda Greenstone

Mattie Stepanek had no ambition for heaven.
Earth for him was an eternally singing white water
Mystery, a school where Harry Potter invented alchemy
Just for him and his stuffed menagerie companions.
All taught him unconditional love. Imagine it!
Not even the wheelchair harness, the filthy tube,
Not that continuous, crotchety, motorized tedium
Could interfere with the mint-edged musical
Score of his sweetsea current which willed, which bore
That unnatural body of his, bloated above useless legs
Yet graced with dancer's arms, fifth position fingers
Which often bled. (Shortly before the end he vainly
Asked the public to pray to halt his bleeding.)

His mother spoke to Oprah through a film of tears,
"I consoled him 'God couldn't possibly want more from
You; God is so very pleased with all you've done.'"
Misinterpreting, the boy feared he had work left to do.
Did she get it? That her son was bargaining for
One more day, one hour, just one minute more
He so loved being above unhallowed ground.

"Hard work keeps the wrinkles out of the mind and spirit." Helena

The Art Gallery
Brenda Kay Ledford

Although it was a chilly morning, I knew spring had sprung. You see, the robins had flocked across my front yard, little purple crocuses popped through the ground and the mountain air smelled like jonquils.

Inside our little red plank house, it was toasty warm. In the corner, a wood heater had a roaring fire and the heat wrapped my body like a blanket. Above the couch hung a tapestry of a big, beautiful sunflower. Sunshine seemed to radiate across our living room.

My sister made the tapestry. She was very talented. Barbara could do anything. She could sew, sing, draw, paint, cook – anything. I admired her and wanted to capture her style of drawing. Since she was still at upper school, I slipped into her bedroom and got one of her charcoal pencils and two pages of drawing paper.

Her records were stacked in the corner. I picked up one and studied Anita Bryant on the album cover. She was so beautiful and I wanted to draw her face. I drew, erased, drew, drew and erased until I got her portrait completed.

Then I picked up another record and gazed at Johnny Cash. He was playing a guitar and I thought he was so handsome. So I decided to draw his picture, too. I drew, drew, erased, drew and drew until I captured his image.

I wanted to hang my portraits in the living room. I put Scotch tape on the back of the pictures and stuck Anita Bryant above the sunflower tapestry. Next I displayed Johnny Cash beside the tapestry.

And I could just hear Johnny singing, "I fell in to a ring of fire.... And it burns, burns, burns. That ring of fire."

I called to Mama who was fixing supper in the kitchen. She came into the living room and looked at my pictures. "Those are really good, Brenda. I'm so proud of you."

I could hardly wait until Barbara got home from school to see my art gallery. I just knew she would really be impressed. The time tick, tick, ticked so slowly. Finally, I heard the school bus and Barbara slammed the screen door as she came into the living room. She froze in her tracks, pointed at my drawings and asked, "What is that? Did you do that, Brenda? Well, we just can't have that in our living room. People will see them and think we're a bunch of poor white trash," and she yanked my drawings off the wall.

Mama heard the confusion and trotted into the living room. She put her hand on her hip and exclaimed, "Girls, I'm not having this! I'm going to put Brenda's pictures up in the house, and nobody better not tear them down," and she gave Barbara a mean look.

My mama rushed into the kitchen, opened a drawer and got the hammer. She dashed into the bathroom and I could hear the hammer pound, pound, pounding. She nailed up my portraits in the bathroom.

When Barbara went into the bathroom, she whined, "Mama, I can't use the bathroom with all those people staring at me. Take them down."

Mama said with a firm voice, "You wouldn't let Brenda display her art in the living room, so it's staying right here in the bathroom. And you better not touch her pictures."

---

the strong man in his wrath!" Elizabeth Barrett Browning ~§~ "I'm

Well, the next Sunday we invited the preacher home to eat. He walked into the bathroom and washed his hands before dinner. He stepped into the kitchen and asked, "Who drew those pictures in the bathroom?"

My face felt hot so I knew I was blushing. I whispered that I drew the pictures.

The preacher said, "Why, Johnny Cash looks real. You're good, girl. Keep up the work."

And that's just what I did.

Wistful Union

Jim Wilson

To see you
Only for a moment
To touch you
Ever so slightly —

Pictures of propriety
Overlaying sweet souls
Cautiously keying
Telegrams of desire

Wild Sugar
Eileen Malone

Of course I remember you, and your birthday, between
the buck and warp of language, we begin to recall markers
it was a dress-up party, mind your manners,
folding chairs tied with bubble-gum pink balloons
on freshly mowed thick lawn
tables with real linen tablecloths, set for little-girl tea

your mother rented a machine to whip colored spun sugar
we took turns, gathered it all up,
wound it around paper cone holders
you called it cotton candy, fairy floss,
but to me it was wild sugar

your hair hung in real curls, honey brown silk, blue satin bow
mine was frizzy home-permed, the color of rotting hay

neither could say what the matter was because we didn't know
what we meant was please, please like me

you were a chiffon-frothed blue butterfly
fluttering at me like a pulse
I whirled you around an inflorescence of crushed daisies
don't know how you put up
with my second-hand horror of a frock
twirling you around and around in a needy, clumsy dance

that you're nasty, cranky, and senile, or that you're always smiling."

nonsense, you say, until then you had been so very lonely
wandering alone through bruised hollyhock and wilted dahlia
never forgot that party, us, dancing
all curly and green in the light

spinning and giggling at how I insisted on calling it wild sugar
pink shreds of sugar clouds sticking silverly to our fingers

it was grand, how you asked me to stay after the rest left
said I could eat as much wild sugar as I wanted

all that bribing; how could we have possibly known
the perfect floating circle of ourselves we were

and here we are, returning to the small satisfactions
talking, taking the soul's way of laying down comfort
refilling the other's little-girl teacup
with sweet grown-up kindness
pouring ourselves out with what could have been, but was not
and purposefully, delicately, drinking of it.

Sonnet for the Young Man I Met at a Mademoiselle Social, 1966
Judith Strasser

My thick glasses removed to a mirrored shelf, blind,
I gave myself to Charles of the Ritz: scissors,
pink foam rollers, style so far from my horn-rimmed
rumpled life that when I emerged from the chrysalis
of dryer/brush-out/spray, put on my specs
and beheld the butterfly, I did not know myself.

That night, you were one of the cast-off suitors
the staff recruited to dance with us Guest Editors.
You held me close, swayed, whispered in my ear
You are the ugliest girl I've ever seen. I fled in tears.
But now that more than forty years have passed
(and I fancy you abandoned by two wives and a mistress
who left once you lost your hair), I see your point, and I
    agree.
That made-over creature was not me, nor who I wished to be.

Fields of a Long Daydream
Roy A. Barnes

In 1977, I began to follow Major League Baseball at the age of ten. I found myself wanting to emulate the homerun hitters of that era, like Reggie Jackson and Dave "King Kong" Kingman. Luckily, the backyard of my home in Casper, Wyoming, was an ideal place to imitate their athletic feats. I taught myself to swing a bat and make consistent contact with a baseball. Most of the time, I used tennis balls, as an airborne cowhide wasn't friendly to windows. I eventually started to hit the ball long enough for it to cross easily over the ivy-covered but unstable wooden back yard fence that resembled the outfield fence in Wrigley Field. Eventually, other kids from around the neighborhood, including my younger brother Raymond, started to gravitate to me whenever I engaged in this activity.

The couple across the alley would often yell at us because the homerun balls landed in their back yard on a daily basis during baseball season. They got really upset if a ball hit and destroyed one of their bedded plants. One spring evening in 1978, as the middle-aged gentleman grudgingly handed me back a batted tennis ball that came close to hitting him, he suggested, "Why don't you guys use Wiffleballs? They usually won't travel as far, so it won't land in our yard as much and kill our plants like baseballs and tennis balls do."

Raymond and I took the man's advice. We purchased some hard plastic Wiffleballs and long, stick-like, but even harder plastic Wiffle-bats with our $2.50 bi-weekly allowances. The Wiffleballs still managed to cross the alley and get into our backyard neighbors' flower beds and patio area, but now they would throw the balls back to us without complaint. I think it started to become a bit of a fun ritual for this couple to spot a Wiffleball somewhere in their backyard haven and toss it back. I even started to visit them when they were outside.

Sometimes I was offered a snack or a cold drink. The man once reminisced about the baseball legends of his day, like Bob Feller, Stan Musial, and Ted Williams. Eventually, we obtained permission to go into their yard anytime to fetch the balls.

We didn't just hit the ball around in my backyard on South Lincoln. Imitation baseball games were played using the Wiffleball equipment. The middle of the yard made up the infield. First base was dwarfed by branches of a cottonwood tree, which often kept batted balls from landing next door, where a ferocious dog lived. The top of a large flat stone, which made up part of the rock walk from the back door of the house to the backyard gate, served as second base. A large prickly bush was deemed third base. Many foul balls got stuck there. Trying to get a Wiffleball out of that bush when it was caught in one of its inner branches could take what seemed like forever. The home plate area in the backyard had really been grassy when my family first moved in. By the end of the first summer, this part of the lawn and the middle of the yard had turned into nothing but dirt. My parents often complained about this. They told my brother and me to quit playing in the backyard so the landlord wouldn't have a reason to evict us. We didn't listen, but surprisingly, the landlord never made an issue of this either.

Whether it was a one-on-one friendly, or a two-on-two playoff match, we kids would really get into some bad spats over calls (we umpired ourselves via shaky consensus), as if our very pride depended upon getting our own way. Raymond and

I had two friends named Richard and Joey who lived down the street from us. Richard was one grade behind me in school while Joey was a classmate of Raymond. These two brothers brought their physically and verbally abusive methods of dealing with each other onto the playing field. Usually, it would be Raymond and Joey versus Richard and me. We older brothers usually got away with forcing our subjective umpiring onto the younger set. Still, many games were stopped over heated arguments between Richard and Joey, oftentimes resulting in contest delays of minutes, hours, or even days, especially on the rare occasions that Raymond and Joey were winning late in the game.

The four of us eventually used our next-door neighbors' backyard (not the ones with the ominous canine) because their backyard infield was more spacious. Homeplate faced the home's green exterior, so that center field to the right-field foul line imitated Fenway Park's fabled Green Monster. To hit a home run anywhere over left center field to the left-field foul line, the ball would have to scale a series of trees and tall bushes that bordered my family's backyard. I'll never forget the milestone that Richard accomplished on that ground. He once slammed seven consecutive pitches for homeruns off of his younger brother, fanning the flames of their already-heated sibling rivalry.

Our Wiffleball games even occurred in the rain. Our blue jeans and t-shirts were so grassy and muddy after nine innings that our clothes were laundered separately from the rest of the wash. I'd even bat a ball around when snow lingered on the ground during wintertime, anticipating the time when the yellow Kentucky Bluegrass turned green again.

The heroic actions of my favorite sports icons shone on through our play in those fields of a long daydream. "Build it and they will come," was the rallying cry of the popular baseball film *Field of Dreams*. Well, the sod in that Casper neighborhood was laid down earlier in the century, and the youth finally arrived. We created in those residential backyards venues where reality was transcended.

Where Am I?

Barbara Darnall

When I was nineteen, twenty, twenty-one,
I based some big decisions in my life
on counsel sought from those
far older (at least fifty or so)
and far wiser
than I.

The calendar says I am sixty-nine.
(I find that hard to grasp!)
If those sages to whom I looked
for their mature advice
were no smarter then
than I am now,

on what wisdom
have I founded my life?

Taking Turns

Betty Jo Goddard

My sister, Mary Lena, always wanted me to play dolls with her. But I wanted none of that sissy stuff. I played cars and trucks or cowboys and Indians with my brother, Jim.

Jim and I took turns killing each other. Behind the garage, among the hollyhocks, we plotted our territory. "You take the west side of the house and I'll take the east," Jim directed. Then we crouched and Jim said, "Ready, set, GO!"

Away we galloped, in a cloud of dust, riding our sticks, slapping our thighs. "Dillup, dillup, dillup, dillup," we shouted. Jim thundered to the east side of the house. I thundered to the west.

When I reached the cherry tree, I leaned my steed against the tree, hid my eyes against the trunk, and counted to a hundred by fives. It was cheating if we didn't count all the way to a hundred. I raced my way to a hundred, blurring twenties into fifties into nineties in a single breath. Done with the count, I leapt into action.

Jumping to grab a limb, I scrambled up that cherry tree. Scraping bare leg against bark, I pulled and hoisted. Higher and higher I climbed. Branches bent and bobbed under my weight. At last. High, high up, hanging onto a waving branch, I shaded my eyes and peered over the roof of our house.

Ah-ha! I spotted the enemy. On the far side of the house, Jim crouched, gun in hand, heading south, sneaking low to get me.

---

indicate where smiles have been." Mark Twain ~§~ "We grow old by

I left skin behind sliding down that cherry tree. My life was at stake. Jim was heading south. I headed north. Converting my trusty steed into a gun, I sped away on stealthy foot. Around the house I crept. Crouched low, heart pounding, scarcely breathing, I closed the distance between the enemy and me.

As I squirmed low, I glimpsed Jim stealing behind the spirea bush. I let out a loud "Yaaah-ha! Surrender or you're dead!" Jim twirled to aim at me and ptowee!, I drilled him. Jim crumpled to the ground.

I raced over and jumped on him. I shook him and poked him and flopped him around. I made sure he was good and dead.

Eyes squeezed shut, Jim lay, limp, unmoving. His eyes barely fluttered when I poked him with my toe. He was dead, all right. I got him.

After a respectable length of time, the dead arose and we went back to our starting point behind the garage. "Ready, set, GO!"

"Dillup, dillup, dillup, dillup!" It was Jim's turn to kill me. And he did. Creeping low, coming around the corner of the house, he'd spot me and he'd get me. He plugged me right in the chest, and I fell – "ahaahahhagh, ohohoho." Staggering to the ground, clutching my chest, moaning a gargley last breath, I died.

So we took turns, Jim and I. When I killed Jim, I felt big and strong. When he killed me, I felt like a hero dying – just like in the movies. I liked it both ways. It sure beat staying inside and rocking dollies to sleep.

Friend of the Family

Al Carty

During the early 1940s, my family lived on a two-hundred acre citrus ranch in the California foothills; my father was foreman of the ranch. The mountains began outside the back door of our little house and wildlife visited the property regularly. Choirs of coyotes sang laments each night from the near hills. Large oak trees grew in our front yard and beyond them was the barn and shop. Next to the shop was our chicken-house, a special attraction for nocturnal hunters. Sometimes wild and hungry eyes flashed from the dark groves.

Occasionally my father or brother would go outside and fire a few shots to drive them further away, but it was seldom necessary. Twenty-four hour security was provided by Ringy, our fox-terrier. Although he weighed less than thirty pounds, he was a fierce offensive fighter and had no fear of any animal, regardless of size. In his capacity as watchdog and general protector he allowed no trespassers. He challenged all who dared come on the property and chased the offenders back to their own regions.

Deer found the bark and tender shoots of young lemon trees a tasty snack and could easily kill an immature tree. Ringy kept this problem to a minimum. As he charged into a group of browsing deer the bucks would turn and stand their ground, heads lowered, trying to hook him with their antlers. Ringy darted in and out, around and under, snapping and barking, somehow avoiding the sharp hooves and horns, and nipped their ankles until the intruders were gone from his territory.

When in the house he was no less alert, and the family learned not to latch the screen door in front of him. If his senses picked up a danger signal his only thought was to get to the enemy and send it packing, and a locked screen would be left in tatters. Coyotes, twice his size, would not approach him singly, but stayed back in the grove in twos and threes, taunting him. He would chase them through the trees and into the hills where the pack waited in ambush. My brother and sister found him one morning lying by the edge of the grove. He had been badly mauled and was barely conscious. They carried him home and prepared a place for him by the kitchen stove. In a few days he was mended sufficiently to limp about the house and stare out the screen door. In another week he was back in action.

My father returned home one afternoon after planting trees on the upper flats behind our house. He noticed white feathers blowing along the ground, and more near the corner of the shop. He found Ringy behind the building with the remains of a chicken between his paws. The blood and feathers on his muzzle left no room for speculation. The dog lowered his head and looked away. My father stood there for a long time, disappointed, angry, sad…betrayed. The loss of the hen was insignificant, but a simple, elemental, taken-for-granted relationship had suddenly changed; a bond had been broken. A partnership had dissolved.

My father picked up the carcass and rubbed Ringy's nose in the gore, speaking to the dog all the while, roughly, tonelessly, the affection gone. He picked up the little fox-terrier and put him in the back of the ranch truck and drove away. He returned several hours later, alone.

We were shocked that our faithful little dog had killed what he had protected for so long, but couldn't believe our father had seen fit to take him away. There was much pleading and crying. He had been a valuable and much-loved family member.

"But Dad, couldn't we keep him in the house?"

"Tom, couldn't we tie him up for a while?"

"I'll keep him in my room, Dad!"

But our father stood firm. "I won't have a dog that kills chickens, or that has to be tied up! I can't trust him anymore and I don't want a dog I can't trust!" So he had given him to a man who owned a small grocery store in Glendora. We missed the dog terribly; we had lost a friend. There was little to smile about for the next few days and we had little to say to our father. He had become an unpopular man.

With Ringy gone the predators began edging closer. My father chased coyotes away the first couple of nights and shot one several nights later. By the end of the week we saw bobcat prints in the yard. Then one evening my father stepped out into the yard and saw the cat clawing at the door of the chicken-house. He threw a rock at it and chased the animal down the trail along the base of the hill. The bobcat climbed a large, dead, pepper tree and spat and snarled from the topmost limb.

My father would have to return to the house for his rifle and a flashlight, for it was growing dark rapidly. He removed his shirt and hung it on a branch, hoping the man-smell would keep the animal in the tree until he returned. The moon would not be up for some time, and he picked his way carefully along the trail back to the house.

As my father pushed shells into the rifle and checked the flashlight, he looked about the house for volunteers. Someone would have to hold the light while he aimed the rifle. My brother happened to be staying the night at a friend's house, so was unavailable. Even had she been asked, my sister would not have gone down that dark trail under any circumstances. And I was too young. My father explained the situation to my mother,

enchanting than the voices of young people, when you can't hear what

and while she understood the need for immediate action, she was less than enthusiastic.

My mother was of a quiet and gentle nature, and enjoyed her family and her role as home-maker. She liked to have things in their places, and to see everyone with his own job to do. At the end of the day's work she enjoyed a book, or the radio, conversation with friends or family, or Chopin, for she was an accomplished pianist. A bobcat up a tree in the middle of a dark night aroused no interest in her at all. But she knew the cat must be dealt with, so she put on a sweater and scarf and followed my father out into the night.

The cat began snarling as they approached the tree. My father put on his shirt and explained my mother's duties to her. She stood a few steps behind him and shined the light up through the branches. The wild-eyed bobcat glared down at her. My father cocked the rifle and took aim. All in one instant the rifled roared and recoiled, the cat sprang from his perch, and the light went out. With darkness all around him, seeing only the muzzle-blast imprinted on the retina of his eyes, my father could do nothing but stand and listen to a screaming bundle crash down through the dead branches and land at his feet. Then it was quiet, except for the sound of running feet behind him.

"And she took the flashlight with her!" This line always drew a big laugh when my father told the story of the bobcat in the tree. It was one of his favorites, and whenever my parents had company, and the cake and coffee were finished, he would point at the gray-and-brown pelt that lay on the hearth and work his way around to that night.

Not long after the incident my father returned from town and parked the truck under the big oak tree. He opened the truck door and Ringy jumped out, ran up to identify each of us, ran to the shop, ran by the chicken-house, then came back to receive pats and hugs. He was very excited, his wagging tail a blur.

When we questioned our father about bringing the dog home, he was slightly hesitant with his answer. "Oh, I was driving through town and looked in the mirror and saw Ringy chasing the truck. I pulled over and let him in." This answer seemed vague for a man who loved a good story, but we were too happy to pursue it further. Our friend was back.

Ringy made his rounds of the yard again and seemed satisfied that things were where they belonged. The chickens were in the yard, scratching and pecking. The dog gave them a wide berth on the way to the house, and turned his head away when one came near him. As he entered the house he began sniffing the air, then worked his nose along the floor. When his investigation brought him into the living room, he bristled slightly at the sight and smell of the bobcat pelt. He circled it a few times, smelling it carefully, then lay down on it. He looked as though the bobcat might suddenly spring up had he not guarded it; from then on he kept constant watch on the pelt.

My father came in from the kitchen with a cup of coffee. He bent down and scratched the dog's back. "Ringy," he said, loud enough for my mother to hear, "you should have been there. You see, I heard a noise out by the chicken-house and went outside to see what it was. Well...."

My mother turned up the music on the kitchen radio and began singing along with it. Then she turned it down and asked, over her shoulder, "Was he mad?"

"Was who mad?" answered my father.

"The man at the grocery store...when you told him you wanted Ringy back."

My father drank coffee, patted the dog, but said nothing. My mother came from the kitchen, drying hands on her apron.

"O.K.," she said, looking at her strangely silent husband, "O.K."

Hobby

Joy Harold Helsing

Second year in retirement
he decides to collect
butterflies

Buys a book of instructions
identification guide
long-handled net
glass-covered display case
pins for mounting
hiking boots
hat to cover his bald head

That whole summer
he traipses fields and hills
stared at by cows
growled at by dogs
laughed at by teenagers
gets lost for an afternoon
tears pants on barbed wire
wanders through poison oak
falls in a creek
is stung by a bee

Manages to catch
a few common specimens

Next spring
takes up fishing

Why Plums No Longer Make Good Metaphors

Rhoda Greenstone

Black plums used to have layers of flavors.
Remember when the skin was so sharp, so rich,
A shiver of recognition caused sweat to pop out
On your upper lip, a mustache of anticipation
For that splashy first bite? Its sour cloak used to
Be so thick it left a heady undertaste that the flesh
Of the cool wet pulp clung to, soothing, coating
The uvula, readying the tongue for that first
Encounter with savory multilinear sweetness.

An initial dip into a bouquet of delicate tastes used
To explode into a fragrant fountain that set off a lust
For a second, third, fourth nibble to get the teeth and
Gums and tongue and cheeks saturated in plum
On the way to the rich, deep red center, that fabulous
Fragrant meat that coddles the plum's stone.
Then, from a mouth crowded with lush sensations,

in happy old age." Victor Hugo ~§~ "The true evil is not the

Purple dribble escaped, spilled down my chin (my lips
Unable to contain the sweet and sour crescendo).

This summer the black plums have thin skin. Tasteless.
Unless it's sour. But mostly it sticks to the palate
Or snags onto a front tooth, an embarrassment
When I attempt to smile (once I even choked on a piece
Of the damned plastic-wrap-textured thing – does that
Sound like an inspiration for good poetry?)
Inside I find a uniformly yellow piece of fruit, one
That has no nuances, no complex flavors, no blush
Of aromatic red paling to pale orange like before.
Nothing to get hung up about. Wasn't it William

Carlos Williams who wrote a famous tanka
(Well, it was famous back when poets read poetry,)
Assuming everyone would get his allusion when
He scribbled, "The plums in the icebox were so sweet/
I ate the whole bowl." I'm paraphrasing. Not that it matters.
Who reads Williams, anyway? More, who remembers plums
So worthy of hoarding, someone would risk getting the runs
Yet still feel guilty about scarfing them down? Those could
Only be a tease on display at Von's or Ralph's. Outer beauty.
Straining today's blank plums into metaphors muddies the
      page
And hardens my already constipated pile of limbic verse.

---

weakening of the body, but the indifference of the soul." Andre

I Loved Lucy

Sally Clark

When I was growing up, one of my favorite rituals was watching *I Love Lucy* with my dad on our black-and-white TV set. Sometimes Mom joined us and sometimes she didn't, but Daddy was always beside me on the sofa in the den. Lucy's antics cracked us up. Desi's accent made ordinary words hysterical and Ethel was Daddy's favorite character, played against Fred's grumpy attitude.

One particular night, I asked my dad a question while we were watching the show. I don't remember what the question was, I just remember he didn't answer me. In fact, he didn't even look at me. I asked again. Still no response. I snuggled up under his arm, waited maybe a minute to see if any words were forthcoming, and then asked again. Still no answer.

This was not like my dad. He always answered me and he always looked at me when he talked to me, except when he was driving. Maybe he was driving, in a sense, that night. All I know is that although his arm tightened around my small shoulders and he held me close, his hand patting reassuringly on my arm, he never said a word.

After a few minutes, true to my childish nature, I forgot my question and turned back to watch the show. Yup, Desi was mad at Lucy again. What on earth had she done this time?

Maurois ~§~ "Character gives splendor to youth, and awe to wrinkled

Many years later, as a grown woman with children of my own, I was visiting my dad when, from out of nowhere in my conscious memory, I recalled the incident on the sofa.

"Daddy, I remember one time when we were watching *I Love Lucy*, I asked you a question and you didn't answer me. Do you remember that?"

His eyes started to crinkle and the corners of his mouth slowly turned up.

"Yes," he said, "I remember."

"You didn't say a word. In fact, you didn't even look at me. Do you remember what I asked you?"

His stomach started shaking like it did when he was about to laugh.

"You asked me why Lucy and Desi slept in twin beds."

"I did?"

"Yes, and I didn't know how to answer you. You were our third child and I was prepared to explain why married people slept in the same bed, but when you asked why they slept in separate beds, you really stumped me. I couldn't think of any way to explain it to you without making sex between married people sound like something negative, so I just hugged you and hoped you would stop asking."

Once again, Lucille Ball's timeless comedy had us laughing. I think she would have loved that.

The Circle Will Be Unbroken
Barbara Breedlove Rollins

The weekend of our parents' fiftieth anniversary my sisters and I, with two of my nieces, sang for our hometown church. I had a twinge of laryngitis but nobody in the family worried about that. They were the singers; I was there for the solidarity. While we tested the sound system on Saturday, the church's music director said he couldn't hear me. As though rehearsed, my three sisters answered in unison, "That's okay."

It took decades for me to realize my voice is not bad – it's just not up to the family standards. I sing at church from the pew and occasionally a stranger comments on my voice. I treasure those moments, but I still know I'm the one of Sam Breedlove's children who didn't get his voice.

Substitutes helped fill the gap. I normally played the piano when Daddy or my sisters sang, though Mary Ellen and Kathy played as well or better. When I was twenty years old, I'd had twenty-one years formal music training: eight of piano, two of organ, ten years in band, and a year's attempt at voice lessons. My saxophone quartet went to state, but I couldn't carry a tune without wandering to another key.

A passion for genealogy only compounded the problem. I knew Daddy's sister was a music major with a powerful voice, that a cousin was a concert pianist, another a professional singer. I remembered Grandmom playing all over the piano keyboard though she couldn't read music, singing to fill the sanctuary as

but a notch in the quiet calendar of a well-spent life." Charles Dickens

she played. As I studied the family I discovered deep roots to the dominant music gene.

In 1942, my grandfather said of his father-in-law, "Death for him was as simple and beautiful as was the life he lived. Quietly, with never a word of foreboding or fear, he slipped through an open door last Sunday morning and now is singing with that magnificent bass voice of his youth in the heavenly choir." Great-granddaddy Richards got his voice through his mother's side of the family. The dominance of great singing as a family trait is recorded the last two hundred years.

Like the final runner on a relay team staring at the baton she dropped, I lamented my ineptitude. The Gaithers recorded a medley of the songs "Daddy Sang Bass" and "Will the Circle Be Unbroken," but the songs had been joined in my mind many years before that. "Daddy Sang Bass" doesn't really fit since Daddy sang baritone and Mother only sang when she taught little children who didn't care how it sounded. Since I only had sisters, "Me and little brother" didn't join right in there. When I did join, my lack of self-confidence shushed me.

On road trips we passed time by singing. A song invariably included was, "When we all get to Heaven, what a day of rejoicing that will be. When we all see Jesus, we'll sing and shout the victory." I guess I've always thought of the family reunion in Heaven as being around a piano, the unbroken circle, Grandmom singing with her grandmother Ray, Richards and Breedloves echoing off the golden walls.

I expect to be at the reunion. I'm guessing somebody else will man the piano. Maybe the new body the Apostle Paul speaks of will include a new voice, a Breedlove voice. I don't know. I do know, though, it's okay that I didn't get Daddy's voice. The circle will be unbroken – the circle here on earth is unbroken. My son was five when he was singled out by the choir director for a solo because he had such a sweet, clear voice and because he carried the tune so well. He sang "The Little Drummer Boy" and went on to sing in the Wesley Foundation Crossbound Choir at A&M. He'll tell you his voice is not great, but I know better. His voice holds the circle together.

Ten-Cent Dreams

Joanne Faries

Held my grandfather's hand
Skipping down the sidewalk while his long legs ambled
Plaid suspenders clung to stooped shoulders
He tipped his shapeless hat to ladies
Shop door clanged and Pop-Pop jangled change
We peered into the pickle barrel and laughed
The green floating wedges looked silly
On a hot day we lingered at the freezer
Discussed the merits of a cherry popsicle versus an ice cream
    cone

Pop-Pop tapped his pipe into a trash bin
Opened a fresh pouch of tobacco
With deliberation, he prepped it
I danced in front of the glass candy jars
Rainbow of wishes, a cavalcade of choices
He dropped a dime into my outstretched hand
I fancied red licorice

Ginny Greene ~§~ *"We are happier in many ways when we are old*

Legacy

Joy Harold Helsing

Over and over
my mother dreamt
she lost her purse

A nightmare born
from dread of growing old
being poor

Nothing could reassure her

Last night I dreamt
my purse was stolen

I set it down
on a shop counter
Then it was gone

Frantic, I roamed the streets
searched dumpsters
followed suspects
asked strangers
if they had seen the thief

Awoke with pounding heart
told myself
it was not her dream

than when we were young. The young sow wild oats. The old grow

The Rivvel Woman
Betty Jo Goddard

When I was small, walking alone at night clutched chill at my back. At any moment, the Rivvel Woman could steal from behind a tree and I would feel the rake of her claws, her long, sharp claws, swiping bloody across my back.

On summer evenings, as soon as we finished supper, my brother Jim and I dashed next door to visit Pearl and Walter, the Edwards twins. We usually found them lounging on their front porch, swapping stories. Pearl and Walter were eighth graders, grown-up and worldly-wise. From their fund of superior experience, they conjured up authoritative stories, awe-inspiring and blood-curdling, to tell us little kids.

One of their stories was about the Rivvel Woman. According to Pearl and Walter, the Rivvel Woman was old, shriveled, and misshapen. She had long claw-like fingers. Her back was hunched, her nose warty, her mouth toothless. She lurked at night. And she always carried a large sack – a sack where she stuffed little kids.

In hushed voices, Pearl and Walter revealed our danger. On dark nights, the Rivvel Woman hid behind a tree, waiting for little kids to come by. As soon as they passed, she jumped out from behind the tree and grabbed them. My imagination finished the story: Her claw-like fingers digging, the fiendish stuffing of her sack, her unseen journey, dragging her prey to her laboratory in back of the cemetery. Then oblivion.

---

sage." Winston Churchill ~§~ "Each child is an adventure into a

I never asked about this laboratory. Oh, no. Not me. Instead, I put my hands on my hips, thrust out my jaw, and said to Pearl and Walter, "Aw, you can't scare me. I don't believe you. I'm not scared of any old Rivvel Woman. Uh-uh! You can't scare me."

Jim and I sat on the Edwards front porch, mouths open, listening to Pearl and Walter's blood-chilling stories. The sky turned gray. Night sounds started. Darkness came and breathed its mystery around the two maples between our house and the Edwards house, two big maples, two dark maples, two maples hiding... who knew what?

Our screen door opened and Mom called, "Ji-im, Betty Jo-oooo. Come ho-ome."

As we turned to leave, Pearl and Walter hissed, "Careful, now. Don't let the Rivvel Woman get you. You'd better run fast or she'll get you for sure." Then they laughed and slapped their thighs.

Jim took off running as hard as he could tear. I stood alone on Pearl and Walter's steps, facing the dark, ominous distance between our house and the Edwards house. I paused, then flounced around to face Pearl and Walter. "Aww, you can't scare me," I repeated. "I'm not afraid of any old Rivvel Woman."

I stuck out my chest and walked down their steps. I left the safe porch and moved into the boding night. Pearl and Walter wouldn't see me run. Nosiree. With fists clenched, chest thrown, legs stiff, I walked. Cicadas hummed, crickets chirped, locusts rasped. A gust of wind, sudden and chill, rustled leaves and other unseen things. Darkness enveloped me. Ahead loomed the first maple tree.

Out of the corner of my eye, I watched the shadows around that tree. Any moment clawy hands might grab me. Shivers tightened my stomach. Tingles ran down my back. My arms prickled with goose bumps. Clutching my elbows hard, I pulled my arms across my chest. I tucked my head and scrunched my bottom, tightening my body forward to elude the sweep of the claw. Stretching my legs, I pounded my heels. Faster, faster. Faster.

Whew! Made it past the first tree. The black bulk of the second tree awaited me. Slap, slap, slap, my shoes hit the sidewalk as I picked up speed. Tense, alert, heart racing, I waited for the grab.

Heels digging, legs thrusting, I passed the second tree and pounded into the home stretch, up our walk, onto our porch, and – whew! – into the lighted safety of our front room. I had escaped the Rivvel Woman once again. And I had walked every inch of the way. Pearl and Walter couldn't scare me. Nosiree!

Booming Late

Meg Pearce

Now that I'm a boomer,
It's time the truth was told.
In my younger days,
I wasn't half so bold.

Today, in my red hat,
I'm quite the fashion plate.
But much like in my youth,
I find I'm booming late!

The Three Ages Of Europe
Janet McCann

Young she was an explorer
jumping nude into languages and oceans
sharing strange vehicles with stranger men
learning European words for hangover:
Katzenjammer, gueule de bois, resaca

Middle-age made of her a traveler
riding the metros without a map
sitting on concrete jetties
eating prosciutto and melon
dangling her feet in the Mediterranean

But now she's just a tourist
following the guide with red umbrella
who herds her along with other sheep
to the bus, or to the chosen bistro where
ready baguettes and coffees line the bar

Aunt Elsie's Telephone

Ruth Sellers

"Hal-lo," Aunt Elsie said into the black mouthpiece of the oak-cabineted telephone. "Yes, I can tell Mrs. Frizzell. She lives about a block away. What did you want me to tell her? Un-hunh. The new dress she ordered from Montgomery and Ward came in and she can pick it up between eight and six. It's how much? $3.98. All right."

Such messages came over that old wall phone several times a day. After World War I, Uncle Henry went to work for the Cotton Belt Railroad. Aunt Elsie subscribed to the telephone service in case he needed to call home should he be unexpectedly detained out of town overnight.

Aunt Elsie's was the only telephone in a three-block radius. She kept up with all the news and passed it on to anyone who wanted to know. Her nature led her to pry into everyone's business, a kind of trade for her, and the telephone served as a tool of that trade.

Her four-party line, the least expensive service offered by the telephone company, allowed her to learn about the Douglases, the Lawhons, and the Barbees. She knew each subscriber's ring. Her ring was one long; the Douglas' two longs; Lawhon's two shorts; and Barbee's a long and a short. She quietly picked up the black receiver from its cradle on the left side of the oak box and held it to her ear to hear the neighbors' conversations.

"What is the worst of woes that wait on age? What stamps the wrinkle

She knew her nature of listening in gave her an edge about what went on in the neighborhood and everyone else on the party line knew it, too. The party line experiences were a little bit like the soap operas of today; they were her entertainment.

The neighbors not fortunate enough to own a phone used Aunt Elsie's in emergencies.

Mrs. Bartels, a neighbor from a block away, came. "Mrs. Bickley, Lewis has a terrible stomach ache, and I need to call Dr. Rice."

"Well, what caused his pain?" asked Aunt Elsie.

"We don't know, but he was up all night with it, didn't eat any breakfast, and feels hot like he has a fever."

"Do you know Dr. Rice's number? The directory hangs there on the wall by the phone." Aunt Elsie stayed close enough to hear the conversation.

"Operator, ring 332," Mrs. Bartels said into the black mouthpiece. "Hello. This is Mrs. Lewis Bartels. Is this Dr. Rice's office? Un-hunh. Can he come out and check on my husband; he has a bad stomach ache. Been up all night with it...He's not in? When will he be back? My husband's awful sick...You say you can get in touch with him on the phone?...Well, he knows where we live. Just have him come on out as soon as he can. If you need to give me a message, call this number, 387. Thank you, ma'am.

"Mrs. Bickley, if Dr. Rice's lady rings, will you let me know? Lewis really needs some help."

"I'll be right here, Mrs. Bartels. Can I do anything for you now? Maybe some chicken soup would help him. I'll kill a chicken and fix him some soup."

Aunt Elsie kept her promise, stayed by the phone and fixed that chicken soup, too. She was just naturally a good neighbor. But if she had been a cat, her curiosity would have wiped her out long ago. She just could not help listening in on the party line.

deeper on the brow? To view each loved one blotted from life's page,

One day she hung up just dying laughing. She hung up to keep from letting Mrs. Barbee know she heard the story about Mr. Barbee and the outhouse mouse.

It went like this. He rushed out of the house to the little building, readied himself to get rid of the water when a mouse ran up his britches leg. He let loose and sprayed the entire interior of the toilet trying to get that mouse out. He unfastened his overalls and came out the door undressing right in the middle of the pasture. He danced the original "Stomp" right there in front of the outhouse. All the time he was shouting a rhythmic, "Oh, Oh, Oh, oh no!"

Of course, Aunt Elsie could not keep this tidbit locked within her head. She shared it with everyone. Not only did her party line rumble, but every party line in the community carried the story. When it came back to Mrs. Barbee, she was mortified.

"I never told anyone but my daughter, Bobbie. How did all these people learn about it?"

"Well, did you tell Bobbie over the phone, Gertie?" Mrs Lawhon asked.

"Yes, I sure did. I should have known Mrs. Bickley would hear it. She listens in on everyone's conversations... It is a funny story, though." She broke into laughter when she thought of the sight of Mr. Barbee trying to get rid of that mouse.

In spite of Aunt Elsie's listening to everyone on the party line, everyone in the community loved her. Her natural giving spirit prompted her to help all the people. If anyone was sick, she prepared food for them and did what she could to help them mend. So, in a way, her good nature of helping and her less desirable nature of being a busybody balanced out each other. No one seemed to think any less of this good woman for eavesdropping on telephone conversations. Not only did she take messages, she often made calls for people hesitant about using the unfamiliar telephone. Without her phone, she might

---

And be alone on earth, as I am now." Lord Byron ~§~ "Of all the

never have known when someone needed her help, and it was
her nature to offer that, too.

That old phone served the community well because of Aunt
Elsie's service to others through eavesdropping on the party
line. Today's communication services lack the personal touch
of Aunt Elsie's old oak telephone that hung on the wall, and
when she rang "Central," a real person answered.

The Gate

Barbara Crooker

Here is a gate. Since it was discarded,
rusty, unhinged, it locks nothing out,
keeps nothing in. No boys swing on it,
no wind sings through its grate. It leans
against a green shed, divorced from its fence,
its hedge of lilacs, the crushed-stone walk.
Wrought iron filigrees, curlicues.
"What hath God wrought?" I wrote, in the curls
and loops of Palmer cursive, blotching my copybook.
Once, I confused the signals for fire and atomic bomb
drills, stayed huddled on the cool tile of the girls' room,
waited for the all clear, while the teacher searched frantically,
calling and calling my name. Humiliated, my face flamed
     every shade
of red, from Brick to Maroon to Indian, those politically
     incorrect
days. I worried, would my scarred wooden desk be enough

---

barbarous middle ages, that which is most barbarous is the middle age

protection if the bomb landed on it? We saw the bombs
    bursting in air
on the fourth of July, and knew they were no bigger than our
    hands.
We ducked and covered, did as we were told. Later that year,
we would be Polio Pioneers, roll up our sleeves to test the
    Salk
Vaccine, line up in blind faith for our shot in the dark.
The Cold War blazed on. Elvis swiveled his hips, Little
    Richard
put on eye liner, and rock 'n roll was born. We wrote our
    secrets
in diaries, powder-puff vinyl covers, tiny silver keys. The
    future
seemed to be locked in place, latches clicking, doors closing,
but then a gate swung open to the rainbow garden of the
    sixties,
and nothing would ever be the same.

Letting Go

SuzAnne C. Cole

Butterfly – orange, black
defined in white —
alights on my leg;
as impossible to hold
as the adult children
sharing this holiday.

---

of man!" Lord Byron ~§~ "Children's talent to endure stems from

Nearing Menopause, I Run into Elvis at Shoprite

Barbara Crooker

near the peanut butter. He calls me ma'am, like the sweet
southern mother's boy he was. This is the young Elvis,
slim-hipped, dressed in leather, black hair swirled
like a duck's backside. I'm in the middle of my life,
the start of the body's cruel betrayals, the skin beginning
to break in lines and creases, the thickening midline.
I feel my temperature rising, as a hot flash washes over,
the thermostat broken down. The first time I heard Elvis
on the radio, I was poised between girlhood and what comes
    next.
My parents were appalled, in the Eisenhower fifties, by rock
and roll and all it stood for, let me only buy one record,
"Love Me Tender," and I did.
I have on a tight Orlon sweater, circle skirt,
eight layers of rolled-up net petticoats, all bound
together by a woven straw cinch belt. Now I've come
full circle, hate the music my daughter loves, Nine
Inch Nails, Smashing Pumpkins, Crash Test Dummies.
Elvis looks embarrassed for me. His soft full lips
are like moon pies, his eyelids half-mast, pulled
down bedroom shades. He mumbles, "Treat me nice."
Now, poised between menopause and what comes next, the
    last

dance, I find myself in tears by the toilet paper rolls,
hearing "Unchained Melody" on the sound system. "That's all
right now, Mama," Elvis says, "Anyway you do is fine." The
   bass
line thumps and grinds, the honky-tonk piano moves like an
   ivory
river, full of swampy delta blues. And Elvis's voice wails
   above
it all, the purr and growl, the snarl and twang, above the
   chains
of flesh and time.

Thrift

Joy Harold Helsing

He drives an old car
shops for bargains
wears out his clothes
heats up leftovers
reuses aluminum foil
paper bags
recycles newspapers
bottles, cans
mends, repairs
whatever he can
turns out the light
when he leaves a room
uses even words
sparingly

company in himself and his pursuits, he cannot feel old, no matter

Outhouse Blues

Sheryl L. Nelms

so much of my early
life was spent
suspended

above that black
and gargoyled
pit

hanging there
in the cold ammonia draft

remembering the horror
stories of a cousin
who disappeared
forever

when he was
grabbed
from

below

Snips, Snails and Puppy Dog Tails
Jo Anne Horn

If God created anything more complex, yet more delightful than a boy, He did not share it with us. Boys are a hardy crop and can be found everywhere, growing in wild profusion. They bloom like myriad flowers, each with a special beauty, but together they comprise a wondrous bouquet.

A boy can be a joy, a paradox, a blessing, or, at times, compare only to the seven plagues of Egypt. He consists of many things. He is the happiness of a puppy, the softness of a kitten, the stubbornness of a mule, and the unsullied innocence of the very young. He is the impetuosity of a summer breeze, the unpredictability of a sudden storm, a lump in the throat and a pain in the posterior.

He is a combination of freckles, skinned knees and scabs, held together with Band-Aids. He is too old to be kissed and cuddled, and too young to be deprived of affection. He loves superheroes, chocolate ice cream and spiders – and everything that is bad for him. He hates baths, girls, dancing and church – and everything that is good for him.

A boy is a cacophony of sound. He is shrill in excitement, groaning in despair and bellowing in pain. He can imitate twenty birdcalls, a fire engine, and blast the air with whistles. He can make rude, though innocuous, sounds by instrumentation of his body. These armpit symphonies usually occur at

---

you think it is. You are as old as you think you are." Muhammad Ali

inopportune, embarrassing moments – Mother's bridge parties, Tupperware parties and family reunions.

A boy spills incessantly throughout the early part of his life. He spills milk, soda, the goldfish bowl, and sunshine into the dark corners of our lives. He spills breakfast, lunch, dinner, and laughter, infecting those of us who have forgotten how to laugh.

Without a doubt, a boy is the bravest of hunters. He stalks his prey, either real or imaginary, fiercely and relentlessly. He captures living creatures of all possible size – cats, dogs, frogs and snakes – and stores them in impossible places – the toy chest, shower, Mother's hatbox, and the refrigerator.

The thrill of the hunt is superseded only by a boy's love of demolition. Ah, how he breaks! In the short span of boyhood, he breaks bottles, vases, records, windows, dishes, and many, many mirrors. Later, he will break bikes, furniture, bones (hopefully his own), curfews and hearts.

A boy is a blameless creature, and, therefore, is not accountable for his actions. He blames his brother, his cousin or friend equally and impartially – and often.

"Somebody Else" is a convenient culprit who dwells in almost every household that boasts a boy. "Somebody Else" loses shoes, coats, gloves and books. "Somebody Else" leaves a boy's room in total chaos and the bathroom in shambles. "Somebody Else" wets his bed.

A boy does not deem it necessary to develop an extensive vocabulary. When he is very small, he need only grunt to make his desires known. One grunt may concern anything in the matter of creature comforts. Two grunts may mean all progress made toward potty training has suffered a reversion, and three grunts usually mean the situation is serious and an investigation is in order. At age three, "Why?" is sufficient and seems to serve as a response to any discussion. At eight, the words, "He did

---

~§~ *"For little boys are rancorous When robbed of any myth, And*

it!" will suffice. At twelve, "I don't know" will cover any question a parent may ask on any subject at any time.

A boy is a miniature master of prestidigitation. With unsurpassed dexterity, he can make a multitude of things disappear without a trace – skate keys, one sneaker, the spacer for his teeth, Daddy's pipe, and the cake for Mother's bridge club. With just a smile, he can chase away frowns and change a gray day to gold.

A boy is equipped with a driving personality. He drives, and ferociously, firetrucks, tricycles and bikes. Later, as a teenager, he may drive motorcycles, his mother to tears and his father to desperation.

A boy is a collector of things. He leaves behind him on the road to growing up an assortment of planes, trains, boats, a crooked old kite, and a knife with a broken blade. He leaves behind the gnarled old oak that held him on long summer afternoons. It stands with branches sad, waiting for that boy who will not come again. Tomorrow it will raise its leafy arms to embrace another small boy who will seek its heights.

Too soon this mercurial creation, the boy, is gone. He becomes a tall, young man crossing the bridge to manhood, leaving behind a world of no return. I gaze with pride, but I miss the boy who is gone. He will always be just around the corner constant in my memory, ever-freckled, ever-noisy, and beloved.

Tony
(1954 – 2000)

Powdered Milk

Diana M. Raab

Every year of my childhood
Mother would stack emergency
supplies in our dark basement—

grocery bags of candles, flashlights,
batteries, powdered milk, matches,
peanut butter, crackers, and dried raisins

as if these items could protect us from
the reason for the weekly grade school
drills which no one explained,

of hiding under our desks for protection
in case of emergency. I knew nothing
else would matter, but me grabbing

my favorite Tiny Tears doll
for the very last time, before
we had to whisper good-bye because

some indescribable force of nature
could have possibly decided
there was a better place for us both.

Gumming of Age in the Bronx
Jeanne Holtzman

Back in the days before my 12-year molars grew in, Chiclets were a mainstay of my candy regimen. Of course, they were not the only teeth-rotting treat in those days before fluoride treatments and sealants. I also greedily consumed Bonomo's Turkish Taffy, Jujubes, Junior Mints, Goobers, PEZ, Sno-Caps, Wax Bottles, and 3 varieties of starter cigarettes: red-tipped white candy, chocolate, and bubble gum. But I always came back to Chiclets.

Chiclets offered a full candy experience. You could peek through the crinkly cellophane window and see the shiny little white rectangles that clicked reassuringly inside the thin cardboard box. The first few crunchy bites released a minty-sweet explosion, but the shattered candy shell dissolved too quickly, and left you with the lamentably bland chewy center. I performed rigorous experiments, champing and chawing my way through long summer afternoons before I determined that chewing just one piece was too scanty, not taking up enough mouth-space to be gratifying, but two, or perhaps even three, pieces yielded a satisfying combination of mass, crunch and juice. Other excitable kids I knew chose to empty the entire twelve pieces into their mouths all at once in a giant, unwieldy wad, sugary spit escaping from their straining lips. When the box was empty, you had the fun of blowing into one end to make a cool buzzing sound, kind of like playing a comb. This was

and one of the most difficult chapters in the great art of living." Henri

especially satisfying when joining a box-blowing chorus in the movie theater during a sticky Saturday matinee of cartoons and continuous performances.

But there came a time when I stopped chewing Chiclets. It happened about the same time that Frankie Avalon sang shamelessly about a girl changing from bobby sox to stockings. When I lost my skate key for the last time, let my pink bounce-ball roll down the sewer without bothering to fish it out, and cut off my pony tail. When I started making mandatory monthly trips past the Sweet Shoppe to the drugstore and scuttling home hunched over the embarrassing bulky brown bag. The inevitable time came when I spit out the Chiclets and defiantly snapped my way into womanhood chewing Beech Nut Gum.

Babyish pastimes were replaced by the much more mature activity of walking the streets with my best friend in our adolescent uniforms.

While we didn't need to line up and pass muster in front of a drill sergeant, our regalia was nonetheless subject to rigorous standards. Hair was teased to a predetermined and ridiculous height using a metal rattail comb usually stolen from Woolworth's in a girlie rite of passage. Crop-dusting clouds of Breck hairspray rendered the structure immutable. Dark eyeliner rimmed the eyes in quasi-Egyptian style, with Erace applied under the eyes to camouflage any dark circles. In our regiment, pink lipstick was disdained and lips could be left unadorned, but for those aspiring to true bad girl status, Erace was applied to the lips for a look approaching the cadaveric. The face muscles were slackened into a mask of studied sullenness, too bored even for eye-rolling. Short shorts were topped with a matching shell top. Strapless pumps revealed as much toe cleavage as possible, and the shoe backs were smashed down to allow the required sulky foot dragging. The right hand held a perpetual portable radio up to the ear, and the left grasped a wallet fat with captioned photos and stuffed with the mandatory package of gum.

But the insolent snapping and popping that was the hallmark of our new and sneering identities could never be performed with Chiclets. The gum that was *de rigeur* in the Bronx in 1961 was Beech Nut Gum. This was plain stick gum, in a soft wrapper. No candy coating, no cellophane window, no reassuring click. Just a soft shiny paper package of long thin stick gum, each piece wrapped in an enticing silver foil covered by a paper sleeve that pronounced the brand and could be folded into long chains. This wasn't a baby gum to stuff your mouth with or get stuck in your braids. It was a gum to get caught chewing in school. A taunt in the mouths of the cheap girls with their death stares. A gum with attitude.

It took determination and practice to meet the communal requirements of this army of adolescents. Passing algebra was a breeze compared to mastering the subtleties of hair-teasing, shoe-dragging and gum-snapping. The consequences of failing to fit in, of ineptly imitating the paradigm, were devastating. We knew this instinctively. We couldn't understand why the grown-ups couldn't see it. We wouldn't be caught dead chewing Chiclets. What we didn't really know was that Beech Nut gum was our transitional object, our blankee, our talisman, our mascot. With Beech Nut we could gnash our jaws against the hidden fears that lurked on this mass exodus that we were obligated to make, a journey that we rushed into as much as our chaotic bloodstreams drove us to it.

I left The Bronx when I was 16. Nearly four decades have passed, and I have long since forgotten my teasing comb and hairspray. I keep my shoes on my feet when I walk, and I rarely chew gum. But when I do chew, look out! Even though I try to be genteel and ladylike, my mouth cannot unlearn its adamant adolescent lessons. My gum pops and snaps with a defiance I

come from the children, for the children are the makers of men." Maria

have otherwise tirelessly tamed. It seems the old adage is true: You can take the girl out of the Bronx, but you can't take the Bronx out of the girl. Especially not out of the girl's mouth.

Graying in My Life
Michael Lee Johnson

Graying in
my life
growing old
like a stagnant
bucket of
rain water with moss
floating on the top —
Oh, it's not such
a bad deal,
except when
loneliness
catches you
chilled in the
middle of a sentence
by yourself —
ticking away
like an old grandfather clock,
hands stretched straight in the air
striking midnight
like a final
prayer.

Montessori ~§~ "One's age should be tranquil, as childhood should be

Guard Duty

Renie Burghardt

I was eleven when we arrived in the refugee camp in Austria, after having fled our war-torn country, Hungary, in 1947. The camp, located on the outskirts of a small town, was dismal, but at least our immediate needs were taken care of and we were grateful for that.

The people who ran the camp set up a school for the children and organized a scout group. Soon I was a Girl Scout and even went to a scout camp that summer, held in the beautiful Tyrol region of Austria.

The scout camp, located in the wooded mountains of Tyrol, was nicely set up. On one side of a clear, rushing creek were the tents for the girls and our troop leader, Mrs. Kovacs. On the other side, the boys and Mr. Kovacs, the other troop leader, were camping out. But we went for our meals on the boy's side and the nightly campfire was held there as well.

These campfires were always the highlight at the end of the day. We girls, with Mrs. Kovacs, would cross the little bridge that went over the creek and join the boys around the fire, singing songs, telling stories and playing games. All of us had a wonderful time beneath those beautiful, tall, whispering pine trees that covered the entire area.

To teach us courage and responsibility, I guess, our two troop leaders soon devised a plan. Every night, while the rest of the troop trekked across the bridge to the boys' side for the

playful. Hard work at either extremity of life seems out of place."

campfire, one girl would stay behind as the sole guard. This girl was given a whistle in the event she became scared or needed help of any kind, but other than that, she would be alone in the big dark pine woods for a couple of hours. If she blew the whistle, she would be heard and help would arrive within a few minutes, the leaders told us.

Most of the girls, at eleven and twelve years old, were not happy with this arrangement, but voiced their complaints only to each other about it. Nevertheless, the ones who got early turns seemed to do their job well, never once blowing the whistle while sitting in the dark for two hours. But the stories they told each other later, of strange noises coming from the pitch-black woods, frightened the dickens out of the girls who hadn't yet had a turn.

"I heard terrible grunting and I was sure a bear was coming to eat me," a girl named Anna told us as we lay in the tent that night.

"So why didn't you blow the whistle?" I asked, chills running up and down my spine.

"Because I didn't want everyone to call me a chicken," Anna replied. "And I'm glad I didn't. The bear went away after a while. I'm lucky he wasn't hungry."

"I heard strange noises when I was on guard," another girl piped up. "It sounded like a woman crying. I even called out to her, but there was no answer. I decided it must have been a ghost and that she finally went on to haunt someone else. But Mrs. Kovacs said it was probably only an owl. I still think it was a ghost, though."

"I wonder if there are any wolves in these woods?" still another girl asked. "My turn is coming up soon."

"Mine, too," I said, "and I can tell you one thing: If I get scared, I will blow the whistle. I'd rather be called a chicken than be eaten by a bear!"

Thomas Arnold ~§~ *"For God's sake give me the young man who has*

So the following night, my turn to be the guard arrived. Mrs. Kovacs placed the whistle, hung on a long string, around my neck and handed me a flashlight.

"Remember, we'll be just across the creek. If you get scared, blow the whistle," she said, smiling at me. The other girls glanced back at me as they walked away, glad it wasn't their turn. Then they were all gone.

I sat down on a campstool in front of my tent, my heart already pounding too fast, butterflies doing a jig in my stomach. I could see the campfire across the creek and hear the distant singing voices. Everything would be all right, I told myself, glancing uneasily around the now pitch-dark camp and woods. The other girls had survived their two hours as guards, and so would I.

I looked up above the towering pines, and saw the stars and a crescent moon in the sky. I inhaled the wonderful smell of the pines, I began to relax and feel quite good. This wasn't so bad. In fact, it was nice to be alone in the quiet woods, I decided, and I began humming a little tune to entertain myself. Suddenly, I heard a noise. A very loud thump! Thump!

Then it stopped. "Who is there?" I called out. No reply. Then I heard a rustle, followed by more thumps. The noise was getting louder and louder. Again I called out. For a moment there was stillness followed by more thumps. Was my imagination playing tricks on me? I stood up, peered into the woods toward the noise and called out once more. This time the rustling became more frantic and the thumps became louder. There was something or someone out there. It was real, not my imagination and it was heading directly my way!

What if my friends were playing a trick? Would I be the only one to call for help and forever be known as "the chicken?" Resisting the urge to blow my whistle, I tried to think quickly. It couldn't be a wolf, I thought right away. A wolf would sneak up without all that noise. It had to be a bear and it was getting too close for comfort. I hugged the wall of the tent and stared deeply into the woods, the thump, thump, thump growing louder and getting closer. I could feel the vibration each thump commanded. Whatever was coming was large, larger than a small eleven year old girl could handle. It certainly wasn't a ghost, and must be bigger than even a bear.

As I raised the whistle to my lips, the huge thumper of the night came crashing into view and stopped right in front of me. I shined my flashlight on him.

"Snort! Snort!" went the thumper, bobbing his head.

"You're a horse!" I shrieked, spitting the whistle out of my mouth. "A big, giant horse! Hello there, boy. Where did you come from?" I held out my hand as I talked to him. The horse's muzzle touched my fingers gently. He snorted again. I reached up boldly and patted his head.

"There, there, boy. You must be lost or something. I'm sure they'll find your owner in the morning. Meanwhile, you can keep me company. I don't like to be alone in the dark and maybe you don't either," I said as I continued patting him. "Maybe my guardian angel sent you my way, just so I wouldn't be scared."

The horse snorted again. I wondered if I had something in the tent I could give him as a treat.

"You wait here. I'll be right back," I told him, creeping into the dark tent and feeling around for the box of Keks that I had saved. "Here. I think you'll like these, boy." Keks were a kind of cookie-cracker combination that was very popular in Austria at the time, and we had each received a packet in case we got hungry between meals.

The horse did, indeed, like the Keks, and wanted more and more. Soon my package was empty. I walked around the camp boldly now, my visitor behind me the entire time. Noises I heard no longer frightened me. After all, I had a guardian with me. I

"Old age is like everything else. To make a success of it, you've got to

was actually sorry to hear voices crossing the creek as the others were returning.

"Look Mrs. Kovacs, I had company tonight," I called out to them. "So I wasn't alone at all."

"A horse! Look girls, Renie has a horse with her," one of the girls shrieked excitedly as a whole bunch of them gathered around my companion and me.

"Where did he come from?" "I wonder whose horse he is?" "Weren't you frightened when he showed up?" And many other questions followed. Mrs. Kovacs then blew the whistle, and her husband came running across the creek.

"He probably belongs to the farm nearby. We'll check with the farmer in the morning," Mr. Kovacs said, going back to get a rope. "We'll tie him to a tree for tonight."

The following morning, some boys went to the farm, and it turned out that the horse had gotten out of the fenced pasture, and galloped off through the woods. Until he found me, that is!

"I had a horse just like him in Hungary," I told the farmer when he came to get my guardian companion. "I used to ride him all the time. Then we had to sell him because of the war."

"Well," he said, "you can come and ride Rudy while you're here, anytime. He is pretty gentle and he seems to have taken a real liking to you."

And that's what I did. I went to ride Rudy several times before we went back to the refugee camp and all the other girls considered me the bravest of the guards for not blowing my whistle when I heard a thump in the pitch-dark night, in the pine woods of Tyrol.

Poetry Floats

Jim Wilson

I am practicing write and release,
Lifting lines on the rising heat
Of winter's curling chimney smoke;
Laying words out an upstairs window
On a springtime zephyr;

Lofting themes tacked as summer kite tails
Flying to high cotton-cloud pillows while
The slick string slips through my fingers;
Linking fall writings to milkweed seeds,
Lint puffs, and down feathers.

I will float them to you all,
Whomever, whenever, wherever,
And you open them in your time
To read and recite
Till their season is done,

Never knowing me;
Never knowing that I am watching you
From the crack in the closet door universal,
Feeling pleased and planning to float
Verse after verse to you – as our seasons change.

Poppy, Floppy Football Shoes
Doug Sellers

Football became my passion during my high school years as a Wylie Bulldog. The first year I played started off with a bang. The coach came into the classroom and said, "Today you will get your equipment. Check it and quickly suit out." He then dismissed us to go to the gym.

I got my suit but had no cleated football shoes. I went through all the boxes of equipment in the gym and finally found a pair of shoes about four sizes too big. I sat down on a bench and put them on. The laces pulled up tight and made the shoes look really long and narrow. The pointed toes stuck straight up. I walked across the gym floor, and those oversized shoes popped and flopped with each step.

We played our first game the next week on a grassy field at Fair Park Stadium. Pride took hold of our Wylie football team. We ran and played like professionals – we thought. Those shoes of mine flopped and popped all over the field with every step I took. I caught passes and made two touchdowns as I went floppity-pop and poppity-flop across the field.

I caught a pass that thrilled one of the Bulldogs' fans. He called the Coach over to the bleachers and said, "Here's $10, Coach. Get that boy a pair of shoes."

Back in the gym, Coach called me over. I felt nervous, afraid I had done something wrong. He said, "Doug, one of the fans noticed your shoes floppin' and poppin' all over the field. Here is $10 he gave me to give to you so you could get you a good pair of cleated shoes."

I took the $10 to Mackey's Sport Shop the next day and bought a pair of shoes that fit my feet. They cost $9.95. That tickled me good. I felt like I could really play ball now for my Wylie High School Bulldogs.

I proudly kept those shoes until I went into the U. S. Air Force in 1952. Mom and Dad moved during the four years I spent in the military service. I returned home to find both my shoes and two letter jackets gone, but I still have the memories.

Matron

Carole Creekmore

They tricked me into this box –
Dull walls of wrinkles and shadows,
Comfortable elastic waist and roomy seat.

Displayed, but shut up and out,
Seen, but not with their herd –
Only hands free to cook-clean-pay.

Can't find a key or combination –
Can't even find any air holes.
Someone is going to pay!

Borland in the Breeze
Ginny Greene

Most everybody remembers the writer James Michener. But, Hal Borland? His work captivated busy, rushing readers decades ago. His descriptions of the nature he loved made readers feel they were walking alongside him as he pointed out a frog on a lily pad, or a wedge of migrating geese, or an approaching rainstorm.

There may be a few octogenarians who remember the heyday of the man and his writing, but not many. The people who know him best in this century are the high school students who have studied *When The Legends Die* in a lit class. Hal Borland wrote that book and many others. In addition to all his books, several of them for young people, Hal wrote for newspapers and magazines.

Harold Glen Borland came into this world on the prairies of Nebraska on May 14, 1900, and left it from the picturesque fields of Connecticut in 1978. He came into my life through the thousands of words he left lying around on paper. The first selections I found at the library were from his unsigned nature column, one he wrote without a byline for each Sunday's *New York Times*.

His passion ran to describing and defending nature. It led him to commentaries on conservation and preservation and awards from societies. He reviewed Aldo Leopold's book *Sand County Almanac*, commenting on the author's poetic approach

Francis Bacon ~§~ *"Those whom the gods love grow young."* Oscar

to his conservation philosophy, "This book looks as harmless as a toy glass pistol filled with colored candy. It turns out to be a .45 automatic fully loaded."

And then there's the way he expressed his faultless logic. "You can't be suspicious of a tree...."

His collection has led him to be variously classified as a nature writer, an editorialist, a writer in the tradition of a daily almanac, an outdoor writer, a writer of rural America. He, himself, called his columns outdoor editorials.

His motive was simply to write about what he loved. He pitched his idea to the *New York Times* editor because he felt so strongly that city dwellers needed a few minutes to decompress, and a chance to stop and reflect. The essays brought green thoughts to calm those who lived among concrete and high rises. Through his columns, readers sat with him one Sunday on a porch in the warmth of a spring sun, watching a bee bumble past. The next week they walked a sodden path covered with wet leaves, or bent over a busy bug, or watched leaves fall orange and rust and red from a tree. They heard birds chirp, watched wildflowers emerge from the soil, and stood near critters nesting, foraging, raising their young.

Hal Borland's popular column was enjoyed by readers from 1941 to just before he passed away in 1978. Imagine that, now, in this world of hard news, limited space, and rushed readers. No city editor could be coerced to publish such work. Many people considered his column a breath of fresh air in the sooty, noisy midst of New York City.

Some of Hal Borland's 37 years of columns are preserved in a book titled *Sundial of the Seasons*, published in 1964. There is a reformatted sequel, though, for these days. His work is said to read like the weather blogs on the internet. These are written by people who, like me, never knew the writer. Nice to know there's a bit of Borland in the ether.

Mourning Elvis
Betty Wilson Beamguard

They start with the Elvis hype
a week before the anniversary of his death,
show aging fans, female of course,
sobbing at his grave,
twisting soggy tissues,
their faces distorted in grief.

Give it a rest. It's been thirty years,
I say as I watch *The Early Show.*

A few days later, I gaze at the screen
from the bathroom doorway,
transfixed with toothbrush immobile
as they interview Elvis's first love.

She speaks of their innocent kisses;
I dissolve into tears, my lower lip quivering
as I lament their fame-crushed romance
and the loss of my own first love.

burn, old wine to drink, old friends to trust, and old authors to read."

Cruel, Cruel Time
Andrea Zamarripa Theisen

Time has no sense of civility:
it marches on relentlessly,
leaves furrowed tracks upon my face.
Of my sweet youth, there's not a trace.
It stomped my skin with hobnailed boots;
turned it to jelly, and everything droops!
My once-full lips no longer sin
and long black hairs sprout on my chin.
My wobbly legs refuse to dance;
my drain pipes balk. (Could I need Depends?)
My joints protest when I try to walk
and conversation is a matter of luck.
You see, I forget what I started to say,
'cause cobwebs in my brain get in the way.
Any hair that's left is thin and gray
and for all those Big Macs, I've started to pay.
I'm not quite as tall; I've begun to shrink;
my teeth in a glass sit next to the sink.
Time's taking my eyesight just for spite;
while my hearing has flown into the night.
But the vilest deed Time keeps trying to do,
is to snuff out my beautiful memories of you.

Stolen Hymnals

Kerin Riley-Bishop

On the second shelf of the closet at the end of the hallway, in the home I share with my mate and our children, is an old hymnal. It was taken from the forward pew of a Presbyterian Church in Southern California. It was taken accidentally, but unfortunately, and hysterically, this was a common occurrence for my mother and me.

Perhaps Mom was a closet kleptomaniac. Perhaps she so enjoyed song time that she wanted to cherish it through the week. Maybe it was simply her mothering instinct; gathering everything in the recently child-occupied space, to make certain that nothing was left behind. Whatever the reason, we often found, tucked beneath her arm, a hymnal.

Most often, we discovered the "theft" before we got too far, and with cheeks flushed red Mom returned the hymnal to its cubby, or directly to the pastor with an impish apology. I would stand next to her, shaking my head, laughing and giving a chastising look which said Mother! Stealing from a church!

A typical Sunday after church went something like this:

"Mom," I would ask, "What's that under you arm?"

Mother would look at me wide-eyed, toss her hands up, laugh our loud, and trek back into the sanctuary. I was nine when this "tradition" began – it continued through my teens and into my early 20s.

Sometimes I got a jump on things. I would hold the hymnal during worship, or if Mom managed to get it, I would gently take it from her before the end of the service, and calmly slide it back into the nook where it would be able to wait safely for the next parishioner. I always threw Mom a stern glance as if to say, *It's wrong to steal a hymnal, Mother.* Despite my admonishments, more often than not, we would find a hymnal nestled under her arm at the end of the service.

One winter morning we arrived home after church to find that a hymnal had hitched a ride. Mother and I stared horrified at the brown book with gold writing resting in the back seat with our "winter" coats (Southern California winters, cold to us, if no one else) and church programs. I was beside myself! Mother had really done it this time! She had stolen! From a church!

It must have been the extra bulk from the coats that had masked the book. Mom assured me we would return the hymnal the following Sunday. One week turned into two, three, four. The hymnal waited to be returned. Every Sunday, we would come home from church to find it sitting on the table next to the door…where we'd not forget it. It was a very patient hymnal, waiting serenely to be returned it to its rightful place among the other hymnals. I am sure if it could have, it would have laughed at us, forgetful mother and daughter, leaving week after week without it. It was the first thing we saw when we opened the door upon returning home. Once, the hymnal actually made it to the car, but we forgot to take it inside the church, so it rode around in the back seat for awhile.

Weeks and months melted into years. The hymnal became family. We moved several times, Washington state called us home. We packed and unpacked the hymnal, eventually placing it next to our favorites on the bookshelf. *Hymns for the Family of God* found new friends in *Cuffy Bear* and *Cress Delahanty*.

After many cross-country moves, the birth of my son, and a few bad relationships, I finally found someone perfect for me, and settled into a sweet, comfortable life in a hushed West Texas town near my mother. She'd faithfully kept for me all the boxes of my youth and collections I had acquired on my journeys.

One day, my love and I brought the boxes home from storage and I began the emotional process of sorting through my boxed-up past. I opened each one, carefully, for two reasons: I am terrified of spiders and imagined hordes of them jumping out at me for disturbing their homes, and I didn't remember all that I had packed away, and did not want to break anything.

One particular box held a baby doll from my grandmother, an article my father had written on metaphysics many years ago, a tiny newspaper clipping of my father's death announcement, a pink porcelain treasure box with a unicorn on the lid which I had received for my eighth birthday, and...the hymnal. I smiled, remembering how many times we had tried not to leave with it, and how many times we had tried to return it. I thumbed through its pages, recognizing old songs I had loved, humming quietly to myself and even singing a few favorites.

Church is no longer a part of my life, but it is a part of the past which formed me, and memories of those times are held dear. Sundays were for my mother and me. Sunday was the day we set aside to share together. The hymnal is a reminder of who I was and how I became the woman I am. It is a reminder of old trucks with holes in the floorboards; icy winter days, and no heater; warm pie and hot cocoa at the diner after services ended; of living on twenty-six acres by the river and the levee breaking; the smell of apple orchards at harvest; lightning striking too close to the house; wasps falling from their nests in our rafters. The hymnal brings up old memories which might otherwise be lost, some wonderful, some heartbreaking, but all mine.

---

me, old age is always 15 years older than I am." Bernard M. Baruch

Jane

brenda wise byrd

There's a little girl inside of me,
Her name is Brenda Jane.
And she can skate and climb a tree,
And she plays in the rain.

She doesn't have arthritis,
Her fingers are all straight,
And she can run and play all day.
At night she doesn't ache.

She can read a book all afternoon,
Escape to distant lands,
Where she might be most anything.
Her head is full of plans.

And then I see the mirror!
Oh, my, where did she go?
Just what has happened to her?
I'm sure I do not know!

She can't be gone. It isn't fair.
How quickly time does fly.
My hair is gray, my fingers bent,
I ache so I could cry.

~§~ *"Youth is not a question of years: one is young or old from birth."*

But just in case she's still around,
I'll put this red hat on
And do the things that she would do.
My heart is still her home.

For Aunt Marie who still calls me "Brenda Jane."

Carol Lee Turns 60 and I Miss Remembering the Day
Karen Neuberg

She's still my wild
pony, neighing over Brooklyn
sidewalks, though I haven't seen or heard from her
for almost 50 years. Daddy called
her "carrot top" for reasons
obvious to anyone. I miss our pairing
in third grade to stand before the class and tell
stories we made up on the spot about boys
with shiny wagons, red as her hair, faster
than flying horses, but only in their minds.
They never saw her gallop down the block
oblivious in make-believe.
The day she moved to Roanoke
was my first broken heart.

Building Blocks

Kerin Riley-Bishop

I am five.
Today I walked to the grocery store by myself.
I met a friend on the way home.
We walked and talked the five blocks back to the apartments
where he lives too.
Mom got upset when I waved at a man as we left the
driveway tonight.
"Who is that!?"
I hear something in her voice I don't recognize at first.
"My friend."
I tell her we walked home from the grocery store together.
I recognize the tone now. Mom is scared.
Some men do not have good intentions.

I am thirty-five.
Last week my child rode his bike to the convenience store,
his grandfather following in the truck.
My son never walked to the grocery store by himself
at the age of five, or otherwise.
The world is crueler today than when I was a child.
But I am trying to soften
for over the years I have learned...
Some men are heroes.

What Would Dolly Parton Do?
Thelma Zirkelbach

What would Dolly Parton do?

This week my vacuum cleaner died. It was thirty years old, about 120 in vacuum cleaner years, and it had served me well.

I don't know much about vacuum cleaners; in fact, I'm not too fond of them. They signify work. If I had to choose my favorite appliance, it would be a microwave oven. Quick, easy dinners when I'm feeling lazy. Baked potatoes in minutes, not the hour they used to take.

Despite my disinterest in vacuums, I know the name Oreck. Which goes to show the importance of advertising.

I headed to the Oreck store, where a pleasant young man greeted me. I told him I wanted an upright vacuum. "You've come to the right place," he said, grabbed a bag of what looked like feathers and sprinkled some on the carpet and some on the tile floor. Next he dumped a cereal-like substance over them and ground it into the carpet with his heel. He pushed a vacuum toward me and said, "Now, see how easy it is to clean up."

Wow! The vacuum was light, it was easy to move. All the mess disappeared like magic. I was sold.

"We have two models," the salesman said. "This one is hypoallergenic and comes with a ten-year warranty. This has a twenty-one year warranty, and it's HEPA." He explained HEPA meant even more allergenic than hypo-allergenic. I was impressed, but the twenty-one year warranty seemed a bit over-

outward man perish, yet the inward man is renewed day by day." 2

the-top. I'm seventy-two, and I doubt I'll be worrying about the carpets in twenty-one years. Besides, the other model cost $200 less. Easy choice.

Oreck was having a special, which meant they threw in a canister and a free iron. What a deal. I whipped out my credit card and signed up.

"Now," the salesman said, "what color would you like? We have two. Black and red."

Black. Sleek, elegant. A color that belongs in a Park Avenue penthouse.

Red. Who would buy a red vacuum? Dolly Parton?

I stared at the two models, then pointed automatically toward the black.

My hand stilled. Why not choose something out of character, something a little wild? I can't say I'm exactly colorless, but I've always been reticent, a bit staid. I relied on my outgoing husband for support in social situations. But I'm alone now. Perhaps this is the time to reinvent myself, to lead a more vivid life...starting small. It's too late to make myself into a red hot mama, but I could be a red hot vacuumer. The Crimson Granny. Miss Scarlett...in the Living Room...with a Vacuum Cleaner.

"I'll take that one," I said and proudly hauled my sassy new vacuum out to my car.

Corinthians 4:16(KJV) ~§~ "Some of my friends are like freckles.

One Small Step – July 20, 1969
Arlene Mason

I grew up in Seattle, but spent my summers languishing on the banks of the Skagit River in Washington with my parents, as they fished. We spent many weeks camping and fishing with several other people. None had any children, so I was usually left alone with my dog. Together, Missy and I would run through the tall grass and listen to Rock on my big transistor radio.

One day, one of the people who had a camper invited everyone in to watch something on her 9-inch television. By this time I hadn't watched television for over a month; this was going to be a treat. Well, it would have been if there hadn't been ten women in the tiny smoke-filled camper. It was hot and the smell of stale smoke was stifling.

She turned on the television and adjusted the aerial to get the best picture possible. Though it was flecked with static, we could clearly see the cratered surface of the moon. No one breathed as the lunar lander gently settled into the dust. Everyone let out a sigh of relief when it was over.

As we walked back to our campsite, my mother spoke for the first time since we witnessed the landing. "I got a lump in my throat just watching that," she said.

I nodded and never gave it another thought. I did not know I had witnessed something extraordinary.

There's actually no explanation for my affection for them." Owen J.

Remnants

Lyn Messersmith

My grandson has been to the dump.
It's a family ritual; each generation's
version of an archeological dig.
Ancestral prizes are piled on the porch;
symbols of people this child never knew,
or wouldn't recognize without the wrinkles.

The two brothers are here.
This boy bears both their names.
Some faded red tobacco tins
tell tales on Dad. And the
whiskey flask that was
witness to my uncle's life and death.

Containers from nail polish and
perfume mark Mom's last stand
before giving in to washboard,
churn, and rolling pin. Shards
of her best dishes, and surely
a shattered dream or two.

Here are rusty bits of barbed wire
that fenced my grandfolks in.
Blue spackled tin plates and cups,
water keg, wagon wheel hub,

and a cracked crock with no cork,
made to hold moonshine.

Narrow-necked green bottles
from when Coke was just a drink.
A cream separator spout, and
busted yellow Tonka toys,
from a generation of boys
separating my grandson and me.

My grandson's visit is over.
No doubt he should have been
required to return these remnants
to their resting place. Then again,
maybe not. Somehow it seems
too soon to quit this family reunion.

Creamed Spinach
Margaret Fieland

You claimed it was a fine old family recipe
invented by your Grandfather,
the one who owned the inn,
and that he called it
Potspinge
for Potatoes and Spinach.
Which was impossible
now that I think about it
since he only spoke Hungarian.

---

suppose for older people the love of youth in others." F. Scott Fitzgerald

Sugar

Yvonne Pearson

I can say your laugh crumbles
around me like a sugar cookie,
already devoured, I go on tasting.
I cannot speak of the saccharin laugh.
It is no substitute.
Sugaaaaaar. The word
stretched long and sweet
against the heat of your neck.
If our youth was spent preserving —
packing our smiles with salt
in sterilized jars —
let our ripeness now burst reckless
and fall where it may
for sugar is also food.
Let us spend the next twenty years
licking our fingers
know the sweet and the salt
of each other
let the grains of forgiveness
bring us past sixty into
the sweet flush of youth, we are
earth's more now than at twenty.
There is no substitute for sugar.

~§~ *"In youth we run into difficulties. In old age difficulties run into*

The Wedding Bouquet
Karen Karlitz

"Fat, fat the water rat, fifty bullets in your cap," my father sang, staring at my mother's mid-section as she exited their old turquoise-and-white Chevrolet.

"Stop it already, Sidney," my mother said, wrapping her stylish beige cape tightly around her. "No one's laughing." Especially not beautiful Rose, who had put on at least five pounds over the long winter. "I'll lose it in a month."

"You lost it a long time ago, Rosie." My father was in a foul mood because of having to drive all the way to the Bronx for my cousin Marcy's wedding. The people getting out of the Pontiac next to us watched my parents with interest, but my older sister Wendy and I were long past embarrassment over their endless arguing; any subject or perceived slight held potential for them.

Silently we walked toward the catering hall on the Grand Concourse where our Aunt Lily and Uncle Ed were throwing their only daughter and her betrothed, Stewart Baumgarten, a Saturday night affair. Ed, a worker at the Fulton Fish Market, and Lily, a part-time saleslady at Barricini's candy shop, couldn't afford the party, but went ahead with it anyway believing God would provide. Theirs was the side of the family that was religious, the side that hadn't yet moved from their fourth floor Bronx walkup apartment, the side that valued a good education for their children ahead of a closet full of expensive clothing, the side that was looked down upon by my dashing family though such a sentiment was never publicly voiced.

"My father leered at my mother slyly and, like a schoolboy, began to taunt her again. "Fat, fat, the…""

"Shut up, Sidney, you sound like a moron," Rose said, forcing a smile as the Goldman family made its entrance like reigning royalty into the large room.

Sidney wore a new suit that Rose insisted he buy. It was the meat of many of their recent arguments. Thinking it cost too much money – my father was pathologically frugal – he regularly threatened to return it. Wendy, a Rose clone who inherited my mother's clothing gene, was a knock-out in a lavender silk minidress. That bit of DNA skipped my genetic blueprint and left me with a penchant for torn jeans and dirty sneakers, but for weeks Rose lectured me on the importance of wardrobe. She dragged me to her favorite shopping haunts and, when I couldn't bear to try on another dress, got me to agree to a purple velvet mini.

Aunt Lily rushed over to us, her enormous girth clothed in navy blue satin, her sweet face bursting with happiness. "I was starting to get worried. I'm so glad you got here okay," she said.

"You thought we wouldn't?" Rose snapped. Just seeing her jumbo-sized sister made my mother edgier than usual, terrified as she was of becoming truly fat.

Lily let Rose's ill humor pass, and hugged Wendy and me to her enormous breasts. "Come, you're sitting next to us," and she led us to a big, round table next to the dance floor. "I must go see how my Marcy's doing. She's so nervous, you wouldn't believe."

Rose sniffed the air in response. Sidney's eyes darted about the room.

"Where the hell is the bar?" he asked.

The last of life, for which the first was made." Robert Browning ~§~

"I'm sure it's here somewhere," Rose answered, sitting down at the table.

"I'll help you find it," Wendy said, and the two of them went off in search of a drink. A few minutes later, they returned in a huff.

"You're not gonna believe this one." Sidney was livid.

"What?" Rose could care less.

"There is no bar." Sid was horrified. "I drove all the way from Queens and can't even get a lousy drink."

"So?" Rose said.

"Are you kidding me? What kind of affair do your chintzy relatives throw? No booze. I never heard of such a thing."

"They don't drink."

"Does that mean no one else does?"

"It's very inconsiderate," Wendy said, "especially for a Saturday night affair." She lit a cigarette, wondering if anyone would notice if she slipped out to the bar down the street for a half hour or so. Wendy was already dancing dangerously close with alcoholism.

A harried waiter, apparently the same one Sid and Wendy accosted minutes before, rushed over. "Please accept my apologies. There's been a mistake. We do have some white and red wines. I'll bring a bottle of each to your table right away."

"That'll do," Wendy said with a smile.

But Sidney wouldn't let it go so easily. "No vodka! What a bunch of cheapskates."

* * *

Everyone gathered along a makeshift aisle and watched the wedding party make its way to the *chupah*. Wendy, the maid of honor, was three years older than Marcy, and it was a growing thorn in my father's side that his gorgeous daughter had not yet married. He continually harassed my sister about her single state at age twenty-two, and my mother always came to her defense.

"Everybody's youth is a dream, a form of chemical madness." F. Scott

In his darkest moments filled with unbridled fear he'd suggest to Rose, "Maybe she's queer?" but Rose was able to silence him. "Remember Joe?" She referred to the thirty-year-old bartender my sister once loved who caused Sidney to froth from the mouth more times than I'd like to remember. Their prized daughter must marry a professional, a man of substance and money, a man with expensive shoes. If not, what would their friends say? Worry permanently etched its way into my father's face.

The unremarkable hall gamely decorated with all things blue and white was packed with friends and family. Gefilte fish, matzo ball soup, chopped liver, herring, stuffed derma, sweet-and-sour meat balls, brisket with gravy, roast turkey, four kinds of potatoes including latkes, three kinds of noodle pudding, desserts that could choke a horse, it was like the Jewish holidays at the Concord Hotel.

Shortly after the ceremony, the emcee stood atop a raised platform in the dining area. "Now, folks, please take your seats. It is with the utmost pleasure that I present you with our happy couple, Mr. and Mrs. Stewart Baumgarten!" He raised one arm dramatically to the ceiling and bowed.

They pranced onto the dance floor amidst clapping and cheering. Stewart, wiry hair slicked down and sweating profusely, took Marcy in his arms. When the strings of "Moon River" could be discerned, he spun the love of his life around with pride and great joy. Marcy's eyes glistened as she looked at Stewart like he was the only man in the world for her.

"I'll do much better than Stewart," Wendy mumbled, reaching for the bottle of red. But she watched the newlywed couple with a sadness I had never seen on her face before.

The band was awful but everyone got up and danced anyway, even Rose and Sid, who affected the appearance of a happily married couple for the occasion. They did a spirited mambo to a labored rendition of "Tequila." Rose's hips were aflame, Sid's wing-tips were flying. To look at them you'd never believe they'd rather be smacking each other with frying pans.

Wendy seemed distant, or maybe it was the wine. Almost a year had passed since her boyfriend Harry, a man of substance and money who wore Cole Haan shoes, promised to leave his wife. "Any day now," she confided to me, as she whacked down the last of the red.

I felt grateful that I had a few years before my father would start in on me, though his expectations for my mate would be markedly lower. And watching Rose and Sid now in a heated argument near the chopped liver, it was clear marriage wasn't always the best alternative.

* * *

Marcy wore a short blue dress and matching spring coat as she got ready to throw the bouquet; Stewart beamed at her side. Aunt Lily rushed over to Wendy and whispered in her ear, "Hurry, get up, go over there." She tugged on her arm.

My sister took her time walking over to the growing group of women in front of Marcy. She stood on the edge of the gathering feigning indifference. Marcy caught sight of Wendy and hurled the flowers in her direction. But our Aunt Rita, divorced for five years and with no current prospects, leapt across two other hopefuls and grabbed for the bouquet, causing it to ricochet to Table One and land with a soft plop in Rose's beige silk lap. My mother looked pleased; she'd been searching for a wealthy replacement for my father for years.

Some might question a wedding bouquet's ability to determine future nuptials, but it turned out that Harry never did leave his wife, and my sister never married. My mother, however, became a bride for the second time, leaving my father to marry their friend Sheldon, a wealthy Laundromat owner with a striking resemblance to a large Pillsbury Doughboy. As karma would have it, they did not live happily ever after.

one ever has." Anita Brookner ~§~ "What's a man's age? He must

Afternoon at Grandfather's House
Carol Ayer

We drove past oil refineries
in our usual state of discord,
crossed the railroad tracks
in an argument with no caboose.

When we arrived we had snacks —
the cheese,
like the conversation,
too strong for me;
the dip an octave too bitter.

The others ate rum ice cream
while I watched *The Brady Bunch*
in a room long-since abandoned.

I unwrapped a Hostess cupcake,
its artificial taste a reminder
that life, like this day, was only sweet
in make-believe.

hurry more, that's all; Cram in a day, what his youth took a year to

A Dog Named Moshe
Barbara Darnall

My brother and his wife had a dog named Moshe. I guess they thought it was funny that a Czech-Irish Baptist and an English-Canadian Episcopalian would have a German Shepherd named for a Jewish war hero. Moshe transcended both race and denomination, however. He was one of a kind. He had a beautiful head and a long sleek body, but his legs were kind of runty and his ears drooped like a spaniel's, or like he'd just been caught doing something he shouldn't on the carpet. My brother said he was a throwback to the old style German Shepherds who were built lower to the ground than today's breed, but the rest of us thought he had a generous dose of dachshund or basset hound in his less-than-purebred pedigree.

Moshe loved with a fierce love all family, kittens, fresh holes in the ground, babies, and big chewing bones, the dirtier the better. He hated with a fierce hate all sudden movements, stray cats, strangers, loud angry voices, and rattlesnakes – especially rattlesnakes. Whenever he met one of those dangerous reptiles he would bark a peculiar high, chirping bark – my sister-in-law, Regina, maintained he was saying "Snake! Mommy, come quick! Snake!" – and stand guard so that the snake would not escape before she arrived with the gun to dispatch it. Had he wanted to do so, Moshe could have worn many rattles on his collar; he was a great protector of his people and counted much coup.

hold." Robert Browning ~§~ "Perhaps one has to be very old before one

My favorite Moshe story, and there were many, is the one which displayed at once his bravery and his extreme loyalty to his family. It was early spring, one of the first warm days, and Regina was outside with her mother-in-law and the baby, a toddler barely sixteen months old. As the women walked around the yard and talked about planting roses here, and digging a new flower bed there, baby Kirby tottered this way and that, examining the new grass and chortling back at the birds. Moshe watched the baby fondly. As she wandered near the foundation to an older part of the house, he suddenly jumped past her with a growl, knocking the toddler roughly to the ground. Hearing Kirby's indignant cries, Regina turned to reprimand the dog, only to see a huge rattlesnake dangling by its fangs from his lower jaw. The snake had evidently been sunning itself on the old foundation stones when it was disturbed by the baby's presence.

Stunned, Regina acted quickly, handing the unharmed baby to Mary and fetching the gun to shoot the now-retreating snake. Then, she said later, one of those superhuman things happened, the kind you read about where a man lifts a heavy car to free the person trapped underneath. Despite her permanently injured back and slight stature, she lifted the one-hundred-plus pound dog and placed him gently on the front seat of the pickup, and, leaving Kirby in Mary's capable care, raced the several miles into town to the vet, crooning words of love and encouragement to Moshe all the way.

It was touch and go for several days. Moshe's head, kept packed in ice to slow the absorption of the poison, swelled to an enormous size. He reacted sluggishly at first to the antivenom, heaving racking breaths and suffering uncontrollable seizures. Regina stayed with him until they made her go home, saying they would call with any news. The next morning he was still alive, but only just, and all that day and the next his condition did not change. Regina visited him often, and despite his desperately weakened condition, he never failed to thump his tail feebly at the sound of her voice, and to lick at her hand if she came near. At last, the critical period passed, and it was evident that he would live, although he had to remain at the vet's for several more days of recuperation.

What a homecoming! There were balloons and crepe paper streamers, ice cream and tears. It was the very best kind of party for the very best kind of reason: the hero had returned, triumphant, from his ordeal at the hands of the foe. The fair maiden, whom he had risked his life to save, responded with hugs and giggles. Her parents, with choked-up voices, praised the brave dog, gave him new bones and ice cream, and fervently thanked God for his lightning-quick reflexes and unselfish spirit.

Moshe lived a good many years more, until the toddler was past eleven and he himself was old and arthritic. He played his part in the creation of many more Moshe stories, but he never topped this one, nor did he need to. In one blinding moment of action sprung from absolute love, he had secured his place forever in our hearts.

woman past forty should make up her mind to be young; not her face."

Spring Fever
Margaret Fieland

Admiring the pattern the sunlight makes as it filters
through the new leaves,
sparkling on the green grass
and on the sidewalk only recently free of snow,
thoughts floating aimlessly through my head,
I stare out the window beside my desk.

My head cupped in my hand, I sit and stare
at the three-story brick building across the street
curious if the tenants can see into my classroom
just as I can see their living rooms
as I make up stories about them.

I count the minutes until liberation
from my uncomfortable wooden seat,
able to play outside in the sun
and smell the crisp spring air
as I jump rope without my jacket.

My teacher's murmuring voice
is something less compelling
than the world outside my window
as I drift and dream.

Billie Burke ~§~ *"Sadly, freckles speak joy to everyone but the wearer."*

Gathering by the River
Carole Creekmore

Out here in the country where we live, the Eastern Prong Church is the center of all social life. In fact, it is our social life. Sundays, we go to Sunday school and church. Then Mamma talks outside the church until around one o'clock. It takes her that long to be seen by all the other ladies and let everyone just know how deep her Christian charity runs. And though she won't admit it, she also catches up on the latest gossip and shares a bit of her own.

I know when she's about to let some gossip fly about some neighbor or another when her voice gets all whispery and she says, "She's good as gold and I love her dearly, BUT...." That tells me right away that I am going to be standing around for another thirty minutes waiting for her to finish with this neighbor or that one.

Yes, all we do is wrapped around the church. When Mamma is going through one of her sick spells, it's the church ladies that bring us food and whisper about poor Mamma and what a noble saint she is to suffer so. It's pretty clear Mamma suffers a little louder and longer and nobler around them, probably because they bring pretty good food. She also seems to get a little too much pleasure out of lying around and getting me to go for something that's right there in the same room with her, even if I'm not. Of course, she can't go to church when she's sick, but

Daddy and I have to go to let all the ladies know that she's in need of Christian charity, covered dishes, and attention.

She sure lets them know what the others have brought too. I think she likes to play them one against the other to see how much she can get them to compete in what they bring. One spell, she got them up to fresh coconut cakes and churns of homemade ice cream. Daddy was even torn up that time when she got tired of being sick, and usually he's really anxious for her to give up on a spell.

It's just easier most of the time for him to get his snacks at Miss Nora's store near the church. When he takes me, I usually get an ice cream cup with a little wooden spoon and a movie star's picture in the lid. Once in a while when I play with Annie on Sunday after church, Miss Nora even takes us to her store if she needs to count the money in her cash register. We don't have to buy stuff then, because it's Sunday and she's really not open. That way it doesn't count against her being a good Christian and all. It's always nice to play with Annie, even during the week, because we get to stay in the back room of the store while Miss Nora works. When Mamma went into the hospital with one spell, I wanted to stay with Miss Nora, but ended up at Miss Virginia's. It seems what I want doesn't usually matter to Mamma.

There was that time just before Aunt Bertha, Mamma's aunt who took her and her sister in and raised them after their own mamma died, came to live with us. Mamma was working up to a good spell; I can usually see them coming. Right after she realized she'd have to take Aunt Bertha in when she got out of the mental hospital, Mamma got real moody – the first sign. Then she took up sighing and rolling her eyes, the next sign. That Sunday, she sent us to church saying, "You both need the moral training even if I have to suffer alone." I think she had a real dilemma to deal with. She wanted to go let all her buddies see her be a saint about taking Aunt Bertha in, and she wanted to take to her bed for a while. Taking to her bed won out. Guess she figured she might not have as many chances to do that when Aunt Bertha came, so she'd better do it up right while she could.

That was the Sunday I decided to be saved. Most of my friends had already been saved and even baptized, but I hadn't felt that "special call," as the preacher puts it. Joey and Annie had been saved and baptized for several weeks. Donnie June was too, though I wonder about how Christian she was from the way she acted, still pouting to get her way all the time. I was about the only one not saved, and I'm the smartest in the bunch.

I decided, sitting there next to Daddy, that I could work up that special feeling of being touched by the Lord if I put my mind to it, so I started working on it. I tried for that special feeling all through the sermon, the choir's special number, and the invitational hymn. I finally decided during the last verse of the hymn that I must have that feeling I needed to be saved. Tired of trying, I was determined to be saved that day, and I was running out of time. I stepped out of the pew to go down to the front of the church, and I felt Daddy watching me but not saying anything. Joey's dad cried when he went down, but Daddy just looked at me, almost sad. I tried to work up a tear or two all the way down to the front of the church, but all I could manage was a sad, but glad look. It was really solemn when the preacher took the vote to welcome me into the flock, but I was already wishing I'd waited for the real call. It was too late now; I had to go through with it.

After the invitation, I got to stand down at the front of the church with Daddy and get welcomed into the congregation. I felt like some kind of cheat, like God knew what I was doing just to keep up with Annie, Joey, and Donnie June. I wasn't having any trouble keeping that sad look now; I felt downright

---

~§~ *"Age doesn't matter, unless you're cheese." Billie Burke* ~§~ *"You*

awful. The more they shook my hand and hugged me, the worse I felt.

When we got home, Mamma was in a tizzy about all the people who would come over because of the combination of her being under the weather and my religious conversion. She had me cleaning and straightening like it wasn't even Sunday, the day of rest. Once I got the house to suit her, I decided to go out on the porch to think about being a Christian in name only.

I had just about justified my way out of it when Daddy came out and sat in the swing next to me. He asked me kind of quiet, "Did you feel a religious call or just think you should be like your friends?"

I know I looked shocked because it was like he was reading my mind. He's pretty good at that, a lot better than Mamma who doesn't even know what's on her own mind all the time. One thing I never do is lie to Daddy on purpose, so I told him, "I really wanted to be saved and tried real hard for a great revelation or sign…but I'm not sure I got one."

He said, "God doesn't always shout, even though the preacher might make you feel like he does. I feel God a lot more than hear him, and maybe you're the same way. The important thing is to want to be a good person."

I guess I should be shocked that Daddy hadn't felt a great revelation and was satisfied with that. He seemed happy enough for me to be the same way. It sure wasn't like Mamma liked to tell about him, how he used to drink and she and the church saved him. To hear her, you'd think she gave him a great revelation. Guess it goes to show what I really know – and what I don't. After Daddy's talk though, I felt like a Christian. I got to try out my new Christian attitude right away too when Miss Virginia and Miss Nettie drove up at the same time and got out of their cars carrying covered dishes.

Education

J. J. Steinfeld

You sit in the classroom
tapping your fingers on the desk
existential drumbeats
the monotony of angst and despair
and listening to yourself
wondering if God is
kind
generous
vindictive
devious
ethereal
discernible
indifferent
preoccupied
male
female
female-less
male-less
a listener to Mahalia Jackson's gospel singing
or Glenn Gould's playing of Bach
a reader of Iris Murdoch's books
or the writings of Thomas Merton or Hannah Arendt
a fan of Alfred Hitchcock films
or a believer in Disney fantasies

~§~ *"How beautifully leaves grow old. How full of light and color are*

an admirer of Charles Lindbergh's or Amelia Earhart's solo
    flights
or Jesse Owens' speed in front of Hitler.
You raise your hand
and God calls on you
and you ask your question
as usual
not wanting to make a mistake
adverbs and adjectives properly placed, deployed carefully,
that is what you do in the classroom
ask questions of God.
God is disappointed
you're told to stay after school
and write on the board
in your neatest hand
I will not pester the teacher
a hundred billion times.

Wishing Well

Diana M. Raab

Yesterday
I dropped a penny
in that deep orifice
of darkness
pleading for wellness.

Planting By The Signs
Blanche L. Ledford

Daddy and Mama always planted by the signs. They handed the tradition down to me.

I grew up in the Trout Cove near Brasstown, North Carolina. We always had a vegetable garden. Daddy religiously followed the signs in *The Old Farmer's Almanac*.

He and Uncle Joe Lee competed to see which one could plant their Irish potatoes first. We lived on a hill above Uncle Joe and Aunt Clyde, and Daddy kept an eye on their garden.

"Trease," Daddy called to Mama. "Where's the *Farmer's Almanac*? I want to see if it's a good time to plant my Irish taters. You know a feller should never plant them in the foot sign. They would have knots all over them like little toes when you dig 'em up."

Daddy sat in a rocking chair beside the fireplace. Mama's cornbread was baking in the Dutch oven and the aroma filled our little house. Mama fetched the Irish potatoes from the root cellar and they were cooking in an iron pot over the fire.

Potatoes were a staple in our family. Mama prepared them various ways – baked, boiled or mashed. She made potato soup and sometimes fixed patties. We flavored the potatoes with butter, salt and pepper. They were served with deer, bear, squirrel, wild turkey or hog meat. Vegetables such as green beans or roasting-ears, along with cornbread and buttermilk completed our meal.

sun floated to the surface. The more you have, the sweeter you are!"

Since potatoes were Daddy's favorite food, he wanted to plant them early. Mama found the almanac where Daddy left it – in the kitchen cupboard. He flipped the pages and peered over the top of his spectacles at the February planting and gardening calendar for 1933.

"Hot dog!" exclaimed Daddy with his deep voice. "Saturday is a good time to plant the taters. I'll disk harrow the garden on Friday and lay off the rows. Since school's out on Saturday, the younguns can help us put out the taters. This year I'll beat my brother Joe," Daddy added with a chuckle.

Now some folks thought planting by the signs was just superstition, but Daddy lived by the signs of the zodiac and the moon. He was a Baptist preacher and saw no conflict with his religious beliefs. After all, the Bible said in Ecclesiastes 3:1 that there's a season to every purpose under heaven, a time to plant; and a time to pluck up that which is planted.

Ancient astronomers studied the stars and discovered the belt of planets and the moon were divided into twelve parts called "signs." Each of these signs contained a constellation of stars, and each received a name. Since all the signs except Libra were named after living things, the belt was named the zodiac, or "zone of animas."

The twelve signs of the zodiac are Aries, Taurus, Gemini, Cancer, Leo, Virgo, Libra, Scorpio, Sagittarius, Capricorn, Aquarius, and Pisces. Each sign is supposed to rule a certain part of the human body.

All good planting calendars label each day with a sign that rules it. The signs always appear in sequence, beginning with the ram or head, which is Aries and works the way down to Pisces, the fish or feet. The ram appears again and starts a new sequence.

Daddy studied the signs almost as much as he read the King James Version of the Bible. He planted all his crops – onions,

sweet peas, cabbage, corn, green beans, squash and pumpkins –
according to the almanac. Just as he figured out how to outdo
Uncle Joe, someone knocked on the door.

Daddy peeped out the window and there stood Uncle Joe on
the front porch. Daddy handed Mama the almanac. "Hide this,
Trease!" he whispered.

Daddy ambled to the front door. "Well, howdy. Didn't expect
to see you out on such a cold winter day. Come in and sit for a
spell before the fire. Thaw out your toes and nose," he added
with a laugh.

"Don't mind if I do, John. You got your taters planted yet?"
asked Uncle Joe.

Daddy grinned and his blue eyes twinkled. "Why, they're
already leaping out of the ground. I dug 'em last week. Don't
you smell the taters cooking in the pot?"

Uncle Joe snorted and stared at Daddy. He took off his hat
and swiped back his gray hair. Then my uncle pulled off his
jacket, reached into his overall pocket and got a can of Insert
tobacco. He poured the tobacco on a piece of thin paper and
rolled a cigarette. He struck a match on the bottom of his boot
and a ring of smoke blew into Daddy's face.

Daddy coughed and gave Joe a hard look. Smoking and
drinking were two subjects Daddy often covered when he
preached at Copperhill Baptist Church.

Uncle Joe didn't seem to notice Daddy frown. He asked
again, "When are you aiming to plant your taters?"

"Don't rightly know," said Daddy. "It's too cold for a man to
do anything except stay by the fire."

"Well, I got to go," said Uncle Joe. "I expect Clyde has
dinner on the table and she'll be madder than a wet hen if she
has to wait for me."

"Just hang around here," said Daddy. "We'll have a bite to
eat directly."

Robert Browning ~§~ *"The arrogance of age must submit to be*

"Can't stay," said Uncle Joe. "You all come see us," he added and headed to the door with his usual, jerky, bowlegged walk.

Mama walked into the living room and looked at Daddy with raised eyebrows. "Joe didn't stay long," she said. "I was in the backyard feeding the chickens and didn't get a chance to even speak to him."

"I don't think it was a social call," said Daddy. "Brother Joe came for information and left empty handed." Daddy slapped his knee and chuckled.

Mama told Daddy that the contest between him and Uncle Joe was foolish. She also thought telling little white lies was not a good example for the children. Daddy folded his arms and gazed at the flames flickering in the fireplace while Mama talked.

Early Saturday morning, Mama ran us out of bed. "Come eat breakfast," she called. "We're planting Irish potatoes today and will need a hearty meal."

George, Oma, Frank, Mary Lou, Helen and I trudged to the table. It was loaded with food: cathead biscuits, gravy, sausage, scrambled eggs, sorghum syrup and fresh milk. While we were eating, someone knocked at the door. Daddy invited Uncle Joe and Aunt Clyde into the house and asked them to eat with us.

"No thanks," said Uncle Joe. "We've already eaten. Clyde and I have come to help you all plant the taters. If everyone works together, you can get much more done."

Expect Blessings; Expect Joy
Linda Oatman High

I was at the beach, in New Jersey, on my cell phone in a hotel room, talking to my daughter-in-law who wasn't yet exactly my daughter-in-law. She'd been my son's longtime love, his first Girl, and they'd recently moved in together. I'd just had a hysterectomy, ending forever my ability to have babies, and I was mourning the loss.

"I had to take off work today to get a blood test," said The Girl.

"A blood test? What's wrong? Are you sick? You never get blood tests. You hate needles! What's wrong? Are you sick?"

There was a pregnant pause.

"Um, I'm, um, we're going to have a baby," she said.

I gulped. I sat down. I closed my eyes. "Okay," I breathed. "I have to go now, and cry."

And cry I did. I cried for the loss of my own baby-making abilities; I cried for what I worried was the too-soon beginnings of my son's. I worried like crazy. I worried that they were too young. I worried that I was too young. I was only 45; my son was 21. The Girl was 22. Holy cow; I was going to be a grandmother. A grandmother! I knew that there'd be a need for child care, as both parents have to work these days. Should I volunteer? How much would I – could I – volunteer? As an author of books for children, I have a busy career. I write a lot; I travel often to teach writing workshops in schools. How could

future that can possibly console us for not being always twenty-five?"

I go back to changing diapers?! How would I manage my career and a baby? How would we all do this?

The worries continued as the first months passed. I worried about money. I worried about time. I worried about money and time, time and money, in a never-ending circle of concern.

Then one day the phone rang. "Mom?" said my son Justin. "Can you come over? Like right now?"

My heart dropped. "What's wrong?"

"Um, Christine's, uh, bleeding. Spotting. She's hysterical. Can you come over, like now?"

I hung up the phone and once again I cried. I sobbed as I drove – as fast as safety allowed – the 15 miles to Justin and Christine's apartment. I wailed and I prayed, and I prayed and I wailed. I begged God to let this baby – my grandchild – be okay. It was at that moment that I realized how much I already loved this tiny unseen person.

The baby was okay. The spotting stopped, and more months passed. My worries had dwindled, as I repeated my mantra: "This baby will be a blessing and a joy. I love it: the him or her that's my grandchild."

Then one day my cell phone rang again.

"They're taking her in for emergency surgery," my oldest son said.

Again, the familiar drop of the heart. "What's wrong?"

"I...don't really know. They're just saying something about no fluid around the baby."

"I'll be right there," I said.

The baby was born via cesarean section a short time later. He was beautiful, healthy, whole, 8 pounds, 9 ounces of gorgeous baby boy. He was my grandson, and he was perfect.

Connor is now three, and he's a genius: the most spectacular toddler in the universe. I baby-sit him two or three days a week, and we are bonded beyond belief. We are best friends. He calls me M'Mere: a French version of grandmother. I'm not French, but I like the way it sounds.

Justin and Christine had a church wedding last April, and Connor wore a mini-tuxedo, just like his Daddy's. They married in my childhood church, and I had one of those stunning and surreal moments when I was struck by a thought: Here I sit, watching my first baby get married, with his first baby bearing the ring. Wow.

Connor has inspired my writing in new directions. I've created at least a dozen new picture books since his birth, and my first adult book was recently released. Titled *The Hip Grandma's Handbook*, it's a quirky reference book slanted toward the active (and cool) Baby Boomer grandmother. Most of the tips in the book have come directly from my obsessive research resulting from Connor's birth, information gleaned by being a babysitting grandmother who wants to do the best for her grandchild.

Life really does come full circle, and every new life on this earth adds to the magic of humanity. My grandson Connor truly is a beautiful miracle, and this busy writer/mother/grandmother loves him more than words can express.

My lesson? Always expect blessings and joy.

schools of painting, two of architecture and poetry and a hundred in

Chemical Warfare
Suellen Wedmore

My arsenal is point six milligrams
conjugated estrogen, a steadfast hormone
for any slowed soldier, and tretinoin,
(Retin-A) acne's charm, now a truncheon
against wrinkles. There's progesterone, patron
of regular periods. Contact lenses to accent
aging eyes, and who'd have thought zirconium
in a lilac-scented cream a gallant
ally? Miss Clairol keeps one youthfully fair;
for alert eyes there's titanium oxide
blue, and for afternoon slump: caffeine
with Nutrasweet will kick ol' time broadside —
just in time for my birthday dinner when
another candle flames: red dye number #3 and paraffin.

Huxley at the Lobero

Al Carty

The announcement appeared in the *Ventura Star-Free Press* that Aldous Huxley was to lecture, one night only, at the Lobero Theatre in Santa Barbara. My brother read the article with interest, as he enjoyed the differing opinions of philosophy. The good gray philosopher and author would expound on the subject "The Reasons and Meanings of Dreams," or "Why Are Valuable Gems Valuable?" My brother had circled the notice in red pencil.

He called me with this revelation, so I drove down for a visit. He handed me the newspaper, folded down to the small article that contained the glorious news about Huxley's coming appearance.

If the article had promised Louie Armstrong was coming to town, or Buddy Rich, or Cab Callaway, or Benny Goodman, or Laurence Ferlinghetti or even Jack Kerouac, I would have been up for the occasion. But I had never been intrigued by philosophy, (except my own) or the Huxleys. I guess saying you had seen him would count for something, but I wasn't sure just what. Since Bud was not attracted by tinsel and glitter I knew he really wanted to hear what the old boy had to say; evidently I had to hear it too. He said he'd buy the tickets and drinks.

When the time came, I took some time off and drove into Ventura and picked up my brother. We stopped at Swede's place first and drank a few beers; that was all Swede served. It was a

grace, force, fascination. Do you know that Old Age may come after

small place down some side streets outside of town about a hundred feet from the beach. It was early evening and the fog came in on a little onshore breeze and we sat on hard stools. The Swede had a black-and-white television behind the bar, high up. He told us the fights would be on in a couple hours. His wife was going to bring in a big pot of beef stew and pans of cornbread and the people watching the fights were welcome to it, on the house. I was close to saying to hell with Huxley and the Lobero, but Bud was looking forward to it. We told Swede we were going to Santa Barbara to see a movie. We would try to be back for the main event.

We cruised on up the coast and into Santa Barbara and its narrow streets. I pulled my old truck into the parking lot. Very bright overhead lights made the parked cars glitter. I swore. Bud looked at me. "What! What's the matter?"

I smiled and swept my hand in front of us, at the parked cars. There were the finest and newest automobiles that money could buy. This was Santa Barbara, and Aldous Huxley was here, one night only! The Lobero Theatre was where these people gathered, and we were here, too, only not rich. "What the hell," Bud said, "screw'em! We have tickets! Park this ugly thing and let's go see Aldous!"

I pulled the Ford between a dark-green Rolls sedan and a very white Mercedes. My engine galumphed, galumphed. When I turned the key it died instantly, snap! Of all the cars in the lot I doubted if any engine had a tighter compression, but those creations didn't smell like petroleum, either. All the other vehicles smelled like money and leather, and their engines did not galumph, they purred.

We approached the beautiful white stucco theatre and walked through the arched entrance into the hum and warmth of power. The clean smell of the best of everything was in the air. Mingled somehow was the greasepaint and nervous sweat and hopeful presentations of many performers, the dust of the riggings high above the stage, the electric charge that every quality theatre absorbs. On nights when the seats are full, the theatre exudes the magic presence.

The high ornate ceiling was lighted just enough, and the velvet plush and carpeting hushed the splendid atmosphere. We found our seats and settled in. We were already being entertained. We looked about and observed and absorbed because we would be talking about this night for a long time.

Soon the house-lights flickered and important people who were standing began shaking hands and promising to meet later. The Lobero Theatre was rich with history and endowments. Large ladies on spiked heels passed down the aisles, some chattering French loudly, as only certain women can when they want to put on a show of their own. They rolled their eyes and filled the aisles with importance and size and volume, Santa Barbara society at its best. Their names just might be in a column tomorrow.

Huxley knew his audience. If he had been here selling toilet brushes the women present would have exhausted his inventory, for the servants, you know. "Oh, my dear," they would say to their puzzled spouses, "these are from Aldous!"

Finally the great man ambled onstage, the audience exploding with applause and gushing acceptance. His white hair was unruly, his suit charcoal-gray, shoes black, socks white. I thought he looked like an elderly farmer who had wandered into the wrong room at a grange meeting. But this was his room and he knew exactly where he was. He might just as well have walked into a recording studio with a microphone and a few engineers and no audience and, when finished, simply walked off the stage. That was pretty much what he did.

But he did give a presentation. He held a script in his hands, inches from his nose, his sight a longtime weakness, and a

age is not a matter for sorrow. It is matter for thanks if we have left

monotone soliloquy ensued. The audience, for the most part, gave the appearance of being enthralled. With this audience appearance was everything. He rambled on about the dreams he experienced after ingesting cactus buttons in remote regions; the desert areas were not precise. But peyote was the subject and there was no doubt peyote was on his mind. I wondered several times if he might not have some buttons in his pocket.

It wasn't long before curtains parted behind the speaker and a screen appeared. Technicolor slides flashed on the screen showing the white-haired philosopher and others wandering around, going in and out of various tents with sullen-looking Indians watching warily. Huxley was narrating something or other. My mind began to wander and I looked around the room, observing the audience. I saw other eyes moving about. I wondered if some of these richly dressed folks were thinking as I was: "What the hell is this?" It began to feel like a double-feature in the local movie house, when neither film was worth watching. But appearances prevail, and Aldous Huxley was on the stage.

The slide show finally ended, the lecture was winding down, and the meaning of the Meanings of Dreams had not been revealed to me. Later, my brother told me he hadn't gotten the answer either. Evidently the white-haired philosopher had had the dream but decided to keep the meaning to himself. Maybe he just forgot to mention it.

The lecture ended, Aldous Huxley made his uncertain way offstage to thunderous applause. He did not reappear, no curtain-call. A nervous little man in a tuxedo walked out and said the good Doctor was tired and The Friends of the Lobero appreciated the support and please keep on contributing and next week some dance group from Equador or somewhere would be performing. The lights came up and my brother and I looked at each other. Behind us a man said to the woman next

---

our work done behind us." Thomas Carlyle ~§~ "God forbid I should

to him, "What the hell was that about?" The woman shushed him. We all got up and went out of the theatre.

Bud and I stood just outside the entrance and had a smoke. We watched the dinner jackets and gowns pass by, ermines and sables and tuxedos and wonderful, intoxicating perfumes, all going to their gleaming cars. We saw the ermines and sables tighten their lips as they saw their Rolls was parked very near to a 1939 Ford, an uncertain shade of green, accented by several gray primer spots that covered recent body work.

The chauffeurs opened the doors and handed their people into the lighted interiors; the chauffeurs sneered too. The interior lights remained on as the plush machines whispered through the parking lot, the occupants evidently on display.

The engine of the Ford turned over reluctantly for a half-second, about one revolution, and then barked loudly, clearing its throat, settling into its cadence, ta-ta rump, ta-ta rump, galumph, galumph, getting the feel of itself, the special camshaft tickling the valves into their lop-sided rhythm, like Gene Krupa or Buddy Rich making the tentative beginning to a mad solo. Multiple carburetors gargled harshly and waited for action. I kept the baffles closed on the exhaust headers. I didn't want to give any of the remaining gentry in the parking lot heart attacks by blowing raw-fire noise from the side pipes.

We thought about going to the Top-Hat in Santa Barbara for a drink, but decided maybe a beer and beef stew at Swede's would be nearer our style. The old green Ford roared up the coast highway, headers open, screaming, startling and irritating the perfectly normal drivers we passed. We didn't see a cop. Finally I pulled into a space in front of the fog-bound Swede's Place and we went in.

A middle-weight fight was in progress on the black-and-white. A dozen or so people were drinking beer and talking and watching the fight. Swede's wife smiled at us and wiped off a

live long enough to ferment and rot and fall to the ground in a

place at the counter and we sat down. We ate the meaty stew and thick cornbread and drank cold beer and watched the next bout. It was the main event and they were heavyweights and it was a good fight. Swede told us he had once seen Marciano, in Chicago. It was the fight when Marciano had retained the title by whipping Walcott. He, Swede, had been about ten rows back, in person. He said he could hear Walcott grunt when Rocky hit him.

When Swede asked how the movie was that we had gone to Santa Barbara to see, we said it wasn't very good. I thought it sure as hell wasn't Marciano, but I kept it to myself.

Meet Frankenstein

James Penha

Quickly
from the Drake Theater I just knew he followed —
black suit hanging like dead stingrays from his body
clodded boots shuffling with preposterous speed
hands outstretched unbalanced —
he was coming at me
the Frankenstein monster
not really
destroyed by Abbott or Costello or
how could after all I have seen him rise again for two bits paid
       over and over for
the dark of Saturday matinees

squash." Emily Carr ~§~ "An archaeologist is the best husband a

dispatched again by Dracula
who followed him
who followed me home
and when at night I heard the wind I saw
him push the garage door
down and when that settled
down I knew he climbed
up the stairs creaking
when I came home from school
I crept
before I touched my house
slowly on all fours to peek
through the basement window to see if he waited there for me.

I lived in terror every day for years
not a day without Frankenstein in my life
patiently
inexorably
until
one moment impossible to remember
I forgot
about Frankenstein
perhaps when other monsters came by.

Underwater Somersaults
Eileen Malone

At least we can do this, remember
how we were in love with Esther Williams
forcing ourselves to smile like she did
in spite of our eyes burning
from chlorine chops of splashed water

practicing turnovers that took us to the bottom
of things, believing everything turns around
at the end, our wispy hair popping out from under
our caps in tufts and clumps, telling each other
how pretty we were

after the whistle blew and everyone got out
shivering in cold stall showers
we dared ourselves to hide behind the lockers
until the echoes of whistles and voices ricocheting
from cement walls and the entire building cleared out

dared ourselves to slip just us into the lapis blue
gelatin, bodies like mermaids, cause no ripples
or splashes, red hibiscus in our loosened hair
being lifted up and out of the underwater lights
by a helicopter manned with movie cameras
fountains erupting at our feet up to the orchid
garlanded swing where we lean and point our toes

Agatha Christie ~§~ *"Conversation of the old and young ends*

but we just talked, then dressed with the others
hiding behind towels, dabbing Blue Waltz toilet water
behind our ears (that's how our mothers taught us)
we covered our wet pony tails in identical white scarves
applied more Flame-Glo pale pink lipstick
over the darkening reddish-blue it had become
saved our bus fare so we could walk to Woolworth
and cram ourselves into the hollow box and pose
for the photo flash, pucker, stick out our tongues
slide on the tiny plastic seat, fall upon each other
giddy, crazy, laughing, crying, almost peeing our pants

well, more than almost, but that was many lives ago
many girlhoods ago, today we dribble with each cough
or sneeze or unexpected spurt of laughter
husbands dead, children gone, hardly any of us left
we find each other, try to resume where we left off

it seems we have learned much too competently
much too acutely, how to live alone, how to measure
how to avoid other people's hells, save a buck, do without
the kind of friends you just goof around with, can't
remember the last time we caught an old Esther Williams
movie on television, the vanilla scent of cheap toilet water
in heart shaped bottles, the way our dreams swam in sync

oh, we try, but to the whiff of chlorine that comes like
the phantom aroma of snuffed candles one can sense emitting
from a cassette tape of monks chanting just finished and turned
    off
finally one of us becomes sensible about underwater somersaults
and how they come up from under to go over, and over
until they are definitely over, one of us honors the pragmatic
and politely, firmly, asks about grandchildren.

generally with contempt or pity on either side." Samuel Johnson ~§~

Generations

brenda wise byrd

I glanced into the mirror
And saw my daddy's face.
I looked again, but he was gone,
And I stood in his place.

The gleam that twinkled in his eye,
Now sparkles from my own.
I don't know how it got there,
For I'm standing here alone.

His salt-and-pepper wavy hair
Now sits upon my head.
It's curled and rumpled everywhere,
Like he just got out of bed.

His laughter bubbles in my throat,
And gurgles from my mouth.
My accent when I speak, like his,
Is clearly from the South.

He's dead now, but he isn't gone.
I sense him everywhere.
The things he taught still guide my life.
I am his grateful heir.

My Apologies, Sisters
Frances Hern

My ability to fix things extends as far as strips of duct tape or a squirt of WD-40. This is why the sentence, "The front door knob feels loose," recently uttered by my daughter, was enough to spoil my breakfast. I quickly confirmed that the knob was no longer attached to the springy-turny thing and mentally slotted into my day a visit to our local hardware store.

There, I found a handleset on display that was similar to our broken one, but this model was mounted on a left-hinged door. I tried to visualize whether the catch mechanism might be turned around to fit a right-hinged door and, at risk of appearing stereotypically dumb, went in search of a salesman. After a lengthy discussion with a second salesman, the first one told me that it probably could and, if not, I could return the item.

Returns have to be in the original packaging and it took me ten minutes to coax the box open without destroying it. Cheered by this small achievement and the unexpected appearance of my husband, I convinced him that dinner would be half an hour earlier if he took over. I had barely put the saucepans on the stove before he called that the screw hole in the handle was in the wrong place and wanted to know why I had bought an entire new handleset when all we needed was one knob.

"Because you can't buy a knob with a handle," I said. "You have to buy either two knobs or a set like this with knob, handle and a lock too."

explained away by science, but I prefer the explanation that they are

"Then buy two knobs and you'll have a spare," he said, in a tone that implied obvious logic.

"But the knobs might not fit onto our handle."

"Well this one looks as though it will."

The next morning I returned the handleset and bought a set of knobs of the same make. I attached one knob to the old handle and tentatively turned it. The door opened. I turned the knob again at regular speed but as I pulled to open the door the catch slipped back into the jamb. I had to leave for an appointment so warned my son that he would have to open the door slowly and it might take him several attempts, knowing he would need ten seconds, instead of the usual five, to run to his bus stop, several slices of toast in hand. I didn't leave my husband a note. I thought that the slipping catch would be more eloquent.

To my great disappointment, his meeting went on much longer than expected and I tried to install the new catch in a hole that was half an inch too far from the edge of the door. I was repackaging the new knobs and asking anyone who might be listening why such items couldn't be made in one universal size, when he returned.

"But why didn't you buy the same make as our old one?" he asked.

I bit back a retort that this was the make he said would fit, and that this handle screwed on the inside of the door which seemed more burglar proof than our old one with the screw on the outside. Instead I went with the argument that would most appeal to him.

"The old one was the most expensive brand," I said. "If the new one is only going to last three years anyway then I might as well buy the cheaper house brand."

He looked at me as though I had spoken a foreign language. I chose my next words carefully.

"If you came to the store with me you could help me make a more suitable choice."

While I queued to return the knobs, he immediately found a salesman who helped him find an exact replacement of our old handleset, pointed out that it had a lifetime warranty and gave him the phone number so we could claim our refund.

"If you don't know," said my husband on our quiet drive home, "why don't you ask for help?"

He installed the new knob and gave me the job of obtaining a refund.

"Our policy is repair and replacement," the lady said when I phoned the next day.

"But we've already bought a replacement."

I explained that without it we would either be living with a round hole in our front door large enough for someone to insert a bent coat hanger and unlock it, not to mention the brisk flow of frosty October air whistling through our open-plan house, or living with a front door we couldn't open from the inside.

She sighed her disbelief that we couldn't manage such petty problems and told me to mail the receipt and the entire old set to their office. This meant that I would have to have the new lock re-keyed to match our house keys and then install it, or install it as it was and have several new keys cut and distributed before I could package up the heavy hardware and pay the postage to British Columbia. Accurately gauging my frustration level, my husband decided that he would phone the refund department. It was a new day for the warranty representative, or perhaps it was a new representative. When my husband told her that all he really needed was a new knob, a fact I had mentioned when I phoned, she said, "No problem, I'll have one in the mail for you today."

I've thought about why my husband always finds knowledgeable salespeople. I've studied what he says to elicit

---

Francis Picabia ~§~ *"A man's as old as he's feeling. A woman as old*

a response of "yes sir, no problem sir." Even so, my positive response rate is only a quarter of his, though we live in these days of supposed equality. Perhaps I'm conditioned to expect problems and somehow signal to others that refusing to do what I request would be more fun. To counteract this I shall think positively about the outcome of this repair job. Our replacement knob will arrive in time for me to return the purchased set to the store and the staff will have forgotten I have already returned two sets of hardware and will not suspect me of fraudulent behaviour and give me the third degree.

Bridging a Woman's Life
SuzAnne C. Cole

To her husband at first her body is a
bridge of gold drawn up against the hordes.
For her children later, a bridge to the world,
their guide from familiar to foreign,
her strength a footbridge across chaos.

Later, her body-bridge stretched thin
sags as grown children march on. On the other
side the youngest waves, kneels, flares a match.
Weary cross-beams, trusses blaze.

Connie Sue's Concerns

R. Scott Comegys

Connie Sue gets upset if she does not have Chapstick readily available, but crossword puzzles have a calming effect on her. She always keeps a stack of puzzle books in her nightstand, along with a drawer full of brand-name lip balm.

That's because she has numerous stressors, her husband being paramount among them. He says cooking is risky behavior, so he forbids her to do it. He worries she may have a seizure and fall onto the stove. He fears that fire will start in the cat litter box. He is angry about Red Goose shoes. ("They are not half the fun of having feet," he cries.)

"Quit obsessing," Connie Sue has told him, over and over. But he won't seek counseling, and she has grown tired of cold food. She told her new therapist she felt wrung out.

The therapist looked at Connie Sue intently. "What would relax you now?" she asked.

"A new crossword puzzle. Or some doughnuts."

"But the doughnuts would hype you up, wouldn't they? All that sugar?"

"No, sugar calms me down," Connie Sue said. "There's nothing like doughnuts at bedtime. Just boom, puts out my lights."

The therapist frowned and scribbled some notes on a yellow legal pad. "Sounds like you may be hyperactive then. That's

action you can discover for yourself; just rub them on dirty skin.

why we give Ritalin to kids. It's a stimulant, but it slows them down because of their biochemistry."

"I don't believe in that hyperactivity stuff." Connie Sue folded her arms and rested them on her protuberant abdomen. "My first grade teacher always said I was just 'busy,' and she was right. She made me run around the flag pole every morning with a boy named Billy Fowler. We only had 48 states then. I remember because we would stop and help a Cub Scout put up the flag."

"You may well have been living undiagnosed for years," the therapist said. "Adult hyperactivity, it's a cutting-edge diagnosis. Maybe we should medicate you."

Connie Sue shrugged and began to hum "Somewhere Over the Rainbow." Suddenly she sat erect on the sofa and dropped her arms to her sides, the palms of her hands meeting red leatherette. "Judy Garland had problems, and pills just made them worse."

The therapist nodded. "What do you know about her?"

"A lot. *Bonanza* beat her show in the ratings, so she got cancelled."

"Networks were different then."

"And I know about Hayley Mills. I used to collect her pictures."

"Did you see *Pollyanna*?"

"I did. Read the book, too."

"Did you learn anything from it?"

"No. I bet she never walked again."

"She did in the book."

"I know, but get real. She was paralyzed from the waist down, and it was like 1910 or something. Aunt Polly probably just packed her off to Hot Springs every summer for 'the treatment' with the TB people and the polio victims. Can you imagine all of that clanking and crap? And nobody ever got well. Doctors just made up stuff and pretended they were doing something. They still do. You see doctors on billboards now – it's just a big profit scam."

The therapist shifted uncomfortably and glanced at her framed diplomas. "Do you believe that is the general intent of medical practice?" she asked.

"Well, sure. And now that we're on the subject, you remember in the movie, Agnes Moorehead played cranky old Mrs. Snow. She was supposed to be an invalid. The Ladies' Aiders sent Pollyanna over with some calf's-foot jelly, and Mrs. Snow fussed about the doctor."

Connie Sue recalled Mrs. Snow's lines: "All he gives you is pills – just pills and bills, that's all."

"That's a good imitation."

"Yeah, thanks. I'm like an African Grey parrot. I'm a mimic."

"Some might call you a pessimist."

"I wish they'd call me a fatality." Connie Sue reached for her Chapstick. She smeared her lips like Minnie Mouse applying lipstick in a cartoon, with big swipes all over her mouth. "And you know what else? I look younger than I am."

The therapist checked her notes. "Yes, you do look younger than your stated age."

"That's because time is going backwards for me. It's cosmic punishment. I have to live longer than everybody else."

With a glance at her watch, the therapist closed her legal pad in a file folder and clipped her ball point pen to the edge. She smiled. "I believe our time is up."

"No, it isn't." Connie Sue squinted and smacked her lips. "We've only just begun."

---

epidemic leprosy, if anyone should have these conditions." Galen 129-

Considering Nanny's Cookie Jar
Becky Haigler

It is
a funny little jug:
a squatty globe whose only ornamentation is
high-placed curlicue handles and a similar twist of clay
on the lid. The simplicity of form and the age
apparent from the crazed lines of its odd green glaze
are reminiscent of an artifact recovered from the ruins of
some ancient city. And in fact, this jar once cached strange
old treasures. Nanny's cookies were large, soft, formless, and
never-the-same-twice. She didn't put much stock in recipes.
If the cookie jar were found empty by a grandchild's groping
hand, Nanny might be inspired to bake. An invitation to pull
a chair to the kitchen counter and help was even better than
the finished product, and often what I really sought. I don't
keep cookies in the jar now (they're fresher in an airtight
tin) but I love its serene presence in my kitchen.
Smooth and simple, the stolid lines are
timeless as a grandmother's love.

The Red Tide

Anthony J. Mohr

On a warm July day in 1964, Big Louie yelled as he pointed out to sea. "Outside! My God, outside! It's so big. Look at that thing form." Big Louie's eyes had never been so open. The wave built silently and then piped, emitting a throaty rumble lasting almost fifteen seconds before expiring in foam on the beach. "Outside!" referred to waves we could bodysurf. You paced the cresting water, then held yourself rigid, arms straight ahead or at your side. A breathless ride became your reward, uniting you with the inbound tide.

Soupy Sales called us teeners. We were the products of a golden time, the Southern California of 1964. That summer, Gary, Brian, Joe, Eric, Big Louie, Rich and I gave ourselves up to the water. Six weeks from the start of our senior year, we seven were poised to run our high school and finally have some dates before heading east to college. We deserved those dreamy days on the sand. Lying on our blankets, talking about student government and the Johnson-Goldwater match-up as if they were equally important (which they were), we were stoked on teenage success and knew the future lay open, boundless and bright.

A wave was about to break. Joe caught it. I missed and dove under it. When I surfaced and looked back, Joe was rollicking through the foam to the shoreline. In control to the end, he let

---

adolescent." Wendy Cope ~§~ "He is so old that his blood type was

out a victory yell – "Team!" is what he hollered – as he flailed his arms and raced to our beach blankets.

We'd fall asleep until the late afternoon marine layer turned the air moist. Then we scrunched through the sand to our car. The radio blasted all the way to our houses, where we ran upstairs to shower before dinner.

The nights were like velvet. Our bodies became little ovens, giving off the heat we absorbed without sunscreen. We saw *Viva Las Vegas* at a drive-in. The Beatles made us smile and groove. "A Hard Day's Night" reached Number One on the KFWB Fabulous Forty Survey. Their first movie by the same name was due out on August 11. We worried about nothing. Our grades were high. The Democrats were the party of peace and paychecks. Our swimming pools were heated so we could play in them until bedtime.

The red tide arrived in August. Most likely it was an algae bloom, probably nontoxic because none of us got sick. The diatoms made the water glow whenever something – like a swimmer or a wave – stirred them. And since breaking waves stirred them plenty, the surf line became a band of light.

Surfing that band of light sounded like a grand adventure, and on the night of August 4, we decided to try. Everyone gathered at my house. We had just finished piling blankets and snacks in the car when my parents said the President was about to give a speech. At 8:36 Pacific Daylight Time, Lyndon Johnson's face appeared on the television.

He opened with the phrase, "As President and Commander-in-Chief...." The group stiffened. Most of us took civics in summer school. We knew that when the President used those words, military action was coming.

Johnson continued: "[R]enewed hostile actions against United States ships on the high seas in the Gulf of Tonkin have

---

discontinued." Bill Dana ~§~ "A man loves the meat in his youth today required me to order the military forces of the United States to take action in reply."

"It's about time," someone muttered, I think my dad.

"That reply is being given as I speak to you tonight. Air action is now in execution against gunboats and certain supporting facilities in North Vietnam which have been used in these hostile operations."

We were bombing North Vietnam. Everyone in my den supported this long overdue move. So did LBJ's opponent. Looking straight into the TV camera, the President informed us, "I was able to reach Senator Goldwater and I am glad to say that he has expressed his support of the statement that I am making to you tonight."

Certain moments rate as a steeple in your life, the apex of a season. Tuesday night, August 4, 1964, presented such a moment. We whooped through the twenty-minute drive from my house to the Pacific Ocean. The DJ on KRLA said it best: *finally we're showing those Communists what for.* He sounded as ebullient as we felt, racing west toward the red tide. Even better, President Johnson promised that he would get Congress "to pass a resolution making it clear that our Government is united in its determination to take all necessary measures in support of freedom and in defense of peace in Southeast Asia."

Brian was the first to frolic among the phosphorus diatoms. Gary joined him and they swam toward an oncoming shadow, the top of which was a ribbon of lit algae. Before diving under the wave, I saw Brian's head sticking out of the vertical water, his mouth an oval, eyes glaring ahead. For an instant a corona surrounded Brian; then the wave crashed. Brian scored a perfect ride to the beach. So did Gary. Emerging from the glowing froth with his arms in the air and head thrown back, Gary reached for the most awesome syllables at his command to communicate his ecstasy: "Hey, Bamboola!"

---

that he cannot endure in his age." William Shakespeare ~§~ "Middle

Eric voiced an idea for Student Council as we drove home at midnight. Gary invited us to a swimming party on Saturday. And I decided to ask out Margie. Braving the red tide gave me the courage to do it. The fall dance was set for September 26. If I called her tomorrow, Margie would have enough notice. It was going to be a sensational senior year.

Family Tree

Becky Haigler

"Becky is a mule's name!" my grandmother said.
She died when I was three.
My "memories" are only photographs.
But I remember what people said about her:
"A saint!"
We have her quilting and embroidery
and her name. But I didn't really know
Mary Elizabeth, my grandmother.
  Mary Ruthe, my mother.
    Mary Rebecca, me.
      Mary Rachel, my daughter.
        Mary Elizabeth, my granddaughter.
There is a strong stubborn streak here.
Are you sure mules don't reproduce?

The Pump Room
Heather Haldeman

"I wonder if the Pump Room's still there?" was the first thing my 79-year-old mother asked. Mom and I were flying to Chicago for a weekend, where we planned to meet my daughter, Hilary, on her college break.

"It was the first fancy bar and restaurant I'd ever been to," she said, reminiscing. "The very first. The night was magic."

"How old were you?" I asked, assuming that she was probably in her twenties.

I should have known better than to assume anything with Mom. "Thirteen," she replied.

Up until my stepfather's death a year and a half ago, my mother traveled extensively. Since then, she hadn't gone anywhere, and the trip to Chicago was a big deal for her. She was so excited, she even renewed her passport. "Mom, Chicago's in the United States. Not to worry."

"But, my husbands always did everything," she replied, referring to her three spouses. "I'm just making sure that I have what I need to get there."

We arrived with plans to visit The Art Institute, take a city tour in a trolley car and see Chicago's magnificent architecture on a river cruise. But, all of this paled in comparison when Mom found that the Pump Room still existed in the Ambassador East Hotel. On top of that, Chicago still allowed smoking in bars.

"Hot damn!" she exclaimed, being a true lover of nightlife.

"Keep on raging – to stop the aging." The Delltones ~§~ "It is not

"My god, there it is," my mother shrieked as soon as the cab turned onto North State Parkway. She acted as if this were her greatest thrill ever.

As our cab pulled up, the doorman leapt to attention and greeted us with a cheery smile. He welcomed us and extended a gloved hand to help Mom out of the cab.

My mother, the consummate flirt, peered up at his nametag as soon as she got out. "Don," she said, "I'm Marilyn." Then motioning to my daughter and me, she continued, "This is my kid and her daughter. They're taking me here for dinner. I'm from California. You know, the land of fruits and nuts."

Bubbling from all the excitement, Mom was in rare form. Hilary and I exchanged glances, and Don was fascinated.

"Can you believe that I haven't been back here in 61 years!" she said to Don, who was obviously impressed.

Digging into my evening bag, I pulled out my camera and asked Don to take a group shot of the three of us with the hotel name prominently featured in the background. "Well, Marilyn, it took you long enough to get back here," he joked, handing back the camera. "We've been waiting."

Don ushered us through the door into the stately old-world elegance of the Ambassador East lobby with its thick marble floors, brilliant chandeliers and ornate high ceiling. Wide-eyed, Mom said dreamily, "Just like I remembered it."

The Pump Room's to your left," Don said, taking Mom's arm like a pro. "But, I'm going to escort THIS piece of history with me." Her blue eyes sparkled and her false eyelashes fluttered.

"Did you know that Chicago's the city of Big Shoulders?" Mom asked, as soon as we were seated at a small table in the bar area. "It's true." She plopped her gold lamé handbag on the tiny table lit by a votive candle. "Carl Sandburg called it that in one of his poems."

Impressed that my mother had read any poetry given the stack of hand-me-down tabloids she passed on to me each week, I nodded. "Really? Gosh, Mom, how'd you remember that?"

"Oh, all the movie stars back in the '50s loved Carl Sandburg."

Angel, the bartender, quickly appeared and took our drink order. Before my mother could strike the match, he whipped out a lighter and gallantly lit the end of her slim cigarette. Mom was in heaven.

Hilary asked if the bar area looked the same. "Did all these photographs of famous people line the walls back then?"

"I don't remember that." Mom tasted the wine. "Ahhh, the first sip. Always the best. Sorry, *excuzzy*." She loved using her bastardized Italian.

"The restaurant part of the Pump Room seems smaller," she said, surveying the area adjacent to the bar. "Like when you go back to your grammar school and the desks look all tiny. But, you remembered them looking big."

After Mom finished her cigarette, we stepped down into the restaurant and snapped a few photos of her in Booth One, where many of the restaurant's famous took up residence. Then, we were seated at a larger table which was more accommodating for the three of us.

"So, Nana," Hilary said, opening her menu. "You were only thirteen? Why were you here?"

"It was the Republican Convention," she mused. "Papa was a delegate and he took me along with him. He was really excited about Wendell Wilke running for President."

A bus boy appeared with water and a basket of bread. Mom strained her eyes to read his nametag in the darkened room. "Ahdbjul?" she asked. Now it was her broken Spanish. "Is that the way you pronounce your name?"

---

hippies don't die, they just lie low until the laughter stops and their

Abdul obliged, saying his name. "Hmmm. Don't recognize that language." Mom shook her head, her frosted bob never moving an inch. "Where're you from?"

"Af-han-ni-stan," he replied, using his native tongue.

Oh dear, I thought, here we go again. Mom is always trying to make a connection wherever she goes.

"Wild," Mom exclaimed. "I've never met anyone from Afghanistan."

Abdul was taken in. "Would you like two pieces of the bread?" he asked her, smiling wide.

Our waiter stood at attention. His nametag read "Joe." Thank goodness. There'd be no new accent from Mom, but she did find out that he was a native Chicagoan.

After ordering, Mom continued her story. "Papa and I sat over there in one of those tables where you sit side-by-side." She gestured to the tables along the wall. "I was wearing a lavender dress with this big purple sash at the waist. It had a puffy slip and I felt beautiful."

Dropping ice cubes into her wine, she continued. "Over there," she pointed to the steps leading back up to the bar, "I'll never forget, two waiters came down carrying flaming skewers of shish kabob. In those days, flaming food was a big deal – cherries jubilee, baked Alaska, that sort of thing. I was hooked. What could be better than this!"

Although there were no flaming dishes on this visit, we all enjoyed our dinners. On the way out, Mom took in the celebrity photos, stretching out the evening as long as she could.

Don waved a cab as soon as he saw us coming. "Marilyn," he called over to Mom, "how was the Pump Room?"

"Marvelous!" Her blue eyes sparkled. Her false eyelashes fluttered.

---

time comes round again." Joseph Gallivan ~§~ "I'm saving that rocker

Helping her into the cab, Don leaned down so that she could hear him. "Now, just make sure that you don't wait another 61 years to come back."

"Not to worry!" she said, as our cab sped away.

Father Lied
Michael Neal Morris

My father lied.
He didn't mean to, I suppose,
but now that he's dead
I have to live with it.

He said, "When you are an adult
living in your own place
with your own children
then you will be the boss."

He said it as if it meant
I'd be in charge, have my way,
run my course
or at least have control of the TV

But when I see his eyes
in my memory they reveal
a pillar of firm despair
going before the ark of hope.

---

for the day when I feel as old as I really am." Dwight D. Eisenhower

Thinking About Red

Janet McCann

The girl's coat in *Schindler's List*
is the first red I remember, and of course
it isn't red, it is just the faintest
suggestion of red, as she is being led
off to be killed, in her absolute innocence,
in her red coat, and why is that
the first red to come to mind, brighter in fact
than all the rest? And then there was
a red dress I had not the nerve to buy
in young womanhood, not wanting
the "wrong kind" of attention, but it was lovely,
the shimmery red fabric under my fingers.
Red blood drops of geranium petals
fell on my front stoop, a middle-class plant
but you saw it; there was a bright red car we hit
because it was hidden in bushes, and you couldn't see it,
it looked like flowers. There was so much blood
when I found a razor blade at three years old
and sliced my fingertip – I shook it,
it rained red over the wallpaper of horses
and carriages – not till then did I scream.
When they said, what is black-and-white
and red all over, I didn't get it;
I thought newspapers had to have red print

hidden away in the middle. There was red
calligraphy on my ankle when I tried
to save the feral cats; I tried to read it.
It healed into a mark my Chinese colleague
said looked something like the word for friend.
Last may be the red of my prom roses.
I had a wrist bouquet. My escort died
years ago, of alcohol and life,
but here's the bouquet, shriveled, in a box
with yearbooks, high school photographs – still red.

Grandma Sult
Michael Lee Johnson

I remember Grandma Salt, or was it Sult,
for her golden silver hair, long
and strung out like a mop.
On mild days tidy and tossed back in a bundle
like twined rope.
If it was Salt it was her hair; if it was Sult
it was German and I know now
where my temper came from.
Standing erect, for her age, 95,
structured posture upright
with a broad smile half the width
of the mouth of the St. Joe River.
She wrote her own history with 11 children.

count a man's years until he has nothing else to count." Ralph Waldo

Little did she know **8** of them would
outlive her. **1** touched the century
mark with a golden pen and added **1** year.
Numbers are important in family histories.
Good genes, then genealogy, grew in fertile ground.
No one knew, hand on the Bible I swear,
where the planting of the seeds originally sprouted.
There was a sense of sternness, and a masculinity
hard to decipher with long dresses on.
They plowed the fields, spanked the butts
of dirty street children; they worked hard
4 the corn they grew and found in their
children's cereal bowl meals.
It is hard to discern all the features
in **1** black and white photograph;
hard to tell what is real and what is
coal smoke tossed, gray from the ears,
to furnaces in the air.
How do you end a poem like this **1**?
I guess I found the answer when my
mother passed away at **98$\frac{1}{2}$**, a fraction.
#'s are important in genealogies these days.

Just Push Play

Ginger B. Collins

Sylvie wasn't on the porch. It was Helen's first clue that something was wrong. Her sister usually paced on the porch or stood in the driveway poised like a sprinter waiting for the starting gun.

Helen rolled to the curb and honked. No response. "Probably dropped dead from a heart attack," she mumbled.

She swung the Buick into the driveway, rocking to a halt just short of Sylvie's garage. She threw the strap of the oxygen tank over her shoulder and using the fender for support, teetered around the car and up the sidewalk.

A blend of Aqua Net and Shalimar sifted through the screen door. Sylvie stood inside, her Clairol blonde in a crisp updo and her lime-green polyester pants suit barely camouflaging her pear shape. She was preaching to the TV, wagging her finger for emphasis. The shiny red of a fresh manicure added fire to her brimstone.

"They'll put you in the home for yapping to the TV like that."

Sylvie waved her sister inside with the other manicured hand, never taking her eyes from the screen. "Look who's talking. You hardly get around on those gimpy legs. If anyone's bound for the home, it's you."

"I'd rather be crippled than crazy."

Helen laughed at her own joke, bringing on the deep, raspy cough of a cat with a hairball. Sylvie stepped forward, but Helen's hand went up like a stop sign. After a few steady draws of oxygen, the cough subsided.

"Don't say a word," Helen said, dropping her hand. "I loved every one of those cigarettes."

She walked to Sylvie's side. "What in the hell are you doing?"

Sylvie turned back to the television, hitting buttons on the remote in a random sequence that brought gray fuzz, charts with arrows, and finally a black screen. "Rita bought me a VCR." Each frustrated word was followed by a stab at the buttons with her red fingernail. "And I want to tape my soaps before we leave for bingo."

Helen rolled her eyes. "Are you still watching that trash? Forget it and let's get out of here. We won't get a good seat if we don't leave now." She grabbed at the remote. "You know it's hard to hear the numbers if we don't sit up front."

Sylvie gave a quick tug. "I've watched *Guiding Light* for over thirty years. I don't want to miss it. That's why Rita bought me this thing. 'So you can get out more, and not miss your programs,' she told me. She promised to get me started. But what happened? She plugged in a few wires, said it was ready, and didn't stay to show me what to do next. Now all I'm left with is a stupid contraption that doesn't work, the rings from her coffee mug on my tabletop, and cookie crumbs on the carpet."

Sylvie went back to pushing buttons. "Don't you have one of these VCR's?"

"I have one but the kids put it together. I just put in tapes and press PLAY."

The words hung in the air. Ernie would have put that VCR together in seconds. But the love of Sylvie's life had been dead

deeply never grow old; they may die of old age, but they die young." Sir

for ten years. Rita, their only daughter, rarely called or visited. Other than Helen and their youngest sister, Vernie, Sylvie was alone.

Helen fiddled with her oxygen hose. "Oh, damn the front row." She unstrapped the portable tank and peeled off her coat. "If my big sister wants those stupid soap operas, we'll put a VCR together."

"Really?"

"Absultootly! Get the instruction book. I'll call Vernie. She'll hold our places. We'll figure this out in no time."

Sylvie was halfway down the hall before Helen finished the sentence. Helen looked at the black plastic hodgepodge of buttons and arrows. It still held the oily warmth of Sylvie's hand. "It's just you and me kid." Helen reached up under the cuff of her blouse for a hanky to wipe Sylvie's hand cream from the crevices. "Make this easy, okay?"

Sylvie returned before Helen got the hanky tucked back up her sleeve. Her face had turned to sunshine and she waved the instruction book like unearthed treasure when she handed it to Helen. "You get started. I'll make coffee."

Helen sat, remote in one hand, instruction book in the other. "Pushy broad." She took a couple of deep drags of oxygen and started reading. From the kitchen she caught the first whiff of fresh coffee. Sylvie was humming "Tennessee Waltz."

In a few minutes Sylvie returned with coffee. It was perfect – that caramel color you get with just a touch of cream. The saucer held two freshly-baked sugar cookies on a folded linen napkin. Helen smiled at the irony. Coffee at her house was "serve yourself" from an old Mr. Coffee – fresh in the morning and bitter by afternoon. And baking? Once Entenmanns's perfected their chocolate chip, Helen stashed away her cookie sheets.

"Any progress?"

"Who writes these books?" Helen asked. "No one our age, that's for damn sure. I look at the diagrams 'cause the words make no sense." She took a bite of cookie and flipped the page. "There's one thing I learned at Theo's hardware store. If you fit the male end of one into the female end of the other, something always happens."

She congratulated herself on the wordplay, then refocused and rotated the book ninety degrees. "Okay, here we go."

"You've figured it out?"

Helen took a few more deep hits of oxygen and slid off the chair. She got on all fours and crawled across to the set. She motioned to Sylvie. "Push the thing away from the wall so I can get back there and undo what's been done. We'll start from scratch."

Sylvie scrambled to the television and put her weight behind the corner. After a few strained heave-ho's, the casters of the metal TV stand rolled across the carpet, exposing a web of black wires that connected the VCR into the back side of the television.

"Where's that fancy magnifying glass of yours? I need to see close up."

Sylvie pulled the pearl-handled magnifying glass off the table beside her chair. "Another helping hand from Rita," she announced, handing it to Helen.

"She means well, Sis." Helen inspected the silver carving on the band. "Nice. Looks antique."

Sylvie puckered her mouth and turned to walk away.

"Where do you think you're going? Get your butt down here."

Sylvie fussed over the potential for wrinkles in her pantsuit as she got to her knees and landed with a thud. There was a symbolic rolling up of sleeves, and work began. They looked at the set and studied the diagram. No kibitzing, no wisecracks, just thirty minutes of concentration as they battled the wires to match up the ins and outs on the two pieces of equipment.

"I think this might be it." Helen's voice had cautious enthusiasm. "Go around front and turn her on."

Sylvie scooped up lint and cookie crumbs from the carpet as she crawled around front. She eased her finger down on the remote's power button as if the level of pressure made a difference between success and failure. The television came alive.

"Okay," Helen called. "Push MENU."

Sylvie gave a gentle push to the button marked MENU and was rewarded with a color grid for "clock set" and "timer set."

Helen peeked around the corner of the set. "What do you see?"

"I think you did it. Come look." Sylvie started to giggle like a kid at Christmas.

Helen huffed and puffed to the front. "Grab my tank, would you, Sis." Her volume was down to a shallow whisper. "I need air."

Sylvie snapped to attention and helped Helen adjust the tank's transparent tubes into her nostrils. The static of the television buzzed as Helen pulled in cool, fresh air. They sat with their backs against the sofa and legs stretched out in front like two teenagers waiting to see Elvis on the *Ed Sullivan Show*. When Sylvie completed the final ENTER, they squealed – then laughed – then cried.

"You did it." She gave Helen a hug. "Thanks, sis."

"Thanks, schmanks. Don't get any bright ideas. I'm not going into TV repair as a sideline." Helen reached for a piece of furniture, starting the long haul to an upright position. "It would cut into Bingo time. Speaking of...let's get going. If Vernie sees a couple of eligible widowers she'll give them our seats and toss us to the back of the room."

childish, as some say; it finds us true children." *Johann Wolfgang Von*

Helen grunted and Sylvie groaned as they struggled to standing. After a quick scan of hair and lipstick, they were off. As Sylvie locked the door, Helen saw her sneak one last look at the VCR remote on the coffee table.

Sylvie got settled as Helen cranked up the Buick. "Let's go for the jackpot today," she said, reaching over to pat Helen on the arm. "I'm feeling lucky."

Free Flow

Larry Lefkowitz

When lads, in summer, we swam in the Delaware river
The last generation before the advent of the swimming pool
Delighting in the river's flow
And moving upstream from King's Rock to Queen's Rock
The water swirling about our waists as we bucked the current
Before the measured pool came to hold sway
With tiled bottom in place of time-smoothed rocks.

Are we different because of it
From the youthful generation that followed?

I leave it to the sociologists or anthropologists
Searching its banks for evidence of the Indians Delaware
Who also tested the river's flow before the Europeans came
Bringing currents of change and rocks no longer named
For the sun and the moon.

The Last Thing I Do
Mary Deal

Passing of the clouds is barely perceptible, unless the boat rocks and disturbs their reflection before the water returns to glass. The landscape is completely calm, not a tree branch bending. Sunlight beats down, felt, and seems the only thing moving.

I sit endlessly, caught up in the serenity of the lake. I think long about the last thing that I must do, but haven't been out on the water since you left. Left, but not quite gone. And this is not the place. I will know when I find the spot, where you and I used to sit and pass the hours as precious time together waned.

I row. We used to take turns rowing. Our favorite game was to try to find the exact mid-point between opposite shores. I never knew where that was but I remember your words: "…just about where the church steeple on the hill comes into view."

Your presence, as always, goes with me even after there is no bringing you back. You can no longer speak to me, but our playful bantering haunts my memories, as does our laughter.

I wait till the water has smoothed again. Then, slowly, I open the urn and set you free from a mind that held you captive and kept us apart yet together for years; set you free to be the liberated soul that you are.

Druid Hill Drive
Terri Kirby Erickson

On Druid Hill Drive,
we were laughing, wiggling
flashes
of mismatched clothes

and spindly limbs,
who spun our parents

in circles as we dashed
in and out of assorted kitchens,
the sound of banging
screen doors loud

as cannon fire, family dogs
barking like mad

from the porch. With bikes
to ride and trees
to climb, forts to build
and bugs

to catch, there were
barely enough hours

in the day for all the things
we wanted to do before
bedtime, when sleep

grabbed us like an undertow,
dragging tired children

to their weary rest
and back again,
for another round
of summer.

Tip Boxes

Karen Neuberg

Betty taught me
to open one more button and bend
while serving men
hot turkey dinners and foamy Coke floats.
She had beautiful, pale breasts
which she lifted and pressed
with her upper arms
as she leaned.

Elsie glided slowly in gum-soled shoes,
plates above her head.
She was a white-haired, red-lipped, powdered twig
who belonged in a room with doilies.
Annie, an apple-cheeked dumpling,
had hands capable of serving
a scoop of ice cream so perfectly placed
it hid the moldy crust on the last piece of pie.

"Nature gives you the face you had at twenty; it is up to you to merit

They instructed me to clean the grill
with seltzer and pumice stone;
to shine the counter and chrome
endlessly with a tired rag.
I opened my second button and let my pale hair fall
across my eye, Veronica Lake-ish.
I put all my tips into the grey metal box with my name
that took its place among the others under the counter.

That summer,
between the end of high school
and the beginning of college,
I read my Suggested Reading,
counted my change, and waited.

Happiness

SuzAnne C. Cole

It didn't take much today
to flood me with joy —
succulent oranges glowing
on a blue pottery plate,
scarlet velvet tulips drooping
over an alabaster vase,
the busy beaks of robins poking
through the debris of winter,
an unsought smile brightening
a familiar face —
may it always be so.

Through Eyes of Love
Elizabeth Simpson

I was nine years old and sweltering in the heat of a Canadian prairie summer when the postman came up our steps on Clifton Street. My father had replaced our storm doors and windows with screens, and I was inside looking out when the postman knocked. His face brightened as my mother moved toward us, and I assumed his smile was in response to her beauty. I'd not yet learned that love has ways of magnifying pleasure in a child's eyes.

My father, whom I looked up to in the physical and metaphorical sense, stood five foot ten, but seemed a giant to me with his curly silvering hair. Neighboring women whispered that he was handsome, but I'd learned to see through his eyes when he praised my mother's porcelain skin and her smiling eyes. As she came toward the door on that hot summer morning, the postman stooped down to tell me my freckles came from catching sunbeams through our screen door. *You've been sprayed with beauty marks*, he laughed, and I believed him.

I was the middle child, padded on each side by a sister who also had freckles, though our parents had none. My mother complained that all her daughters looked like our father. My older sister said it was proof that we were adopted. I told my mother to stand behind the screen door and let the sun freckle her face to match ours. My younger sister toddled away when we stared at her freckled nose and knees.

Though our freckles made clear we were sisters, our coloring differed. My older sister's hair was auburn, and reddish-brown freckles speckled her nose. My hair was dark brown, my cheeks criss-crossed by light brown freckles. My blond younger sister wore pale orange freckles that encouraged the boys to tease her. In grade three she came home in tears. My older sister and I checked our knees before breathing a sigh of relief.

Mother caught rain water to wash the thick curls that rested on our shoulders and then trimmed the bangs over our three broad foreheads. I was in my teens by the time I realized that her complaint about caring for our hair was a mask she wore to cover her pride. *Except for your freckles, you're all like your father*, she would say, a touch of sadness in her voice. It was then I realized the hair surrounding her delicate face was thinner and less buoyant than ours.

Our mother took us to a photographer when each of us reached our ninth birthday. He turned out airbrushed pictures that modified a portion of our freckles. As young adults, we hung these photographs in our separate bedrooms and wondered why our mother allowed him to tamper with reality. By then we had lost our preoccupation with freckles and talked instead of dancing, swimming, and homework.

I was seventeen when I learned that not everyone was as forgiving about freckles as my boyfriend was, this boy I'd met at fifteen and would marry at nineteen. That summer I got a job as a typist for the Provincial Health Services. When a senior official expressed his pleasure in hiring me, I thought he was referring to my typing speed. Instead, he asked me to pose for a poster that would advertise the link between drinking milk and healthy teeth. I walked the hour to and from the office thinking perhaps I might become a Hollywood star. The morning the photographer arrived, I brushed my teeth twice and worked hard to keep my lips from trembling as I smiled into the bright lights from one angle and then another.

My photograph was blown up the size of a kitchen table. Smiling back was the person I saw every morning in the mirror – a girl with perfect teeth. What I didn't know was that I was about to learn the truth in the expression that pride cometh before a fall. *Who would have guessed your freckles would stand out like that?* Mother asked, powdering my face before I left home. *I hadn't realized how many freckles you had*, the senior official confessed. *That's what you get for going to the beach with your boyfriend*, my older sister huffed. *The only beauty that counts is the one that comes from your heart*, my father said. *I love every freckle*, my boyfriend said, kissing my cheeks.

Having failed to be beautiful, I decided to make my mark saving lives. I applied to enter nursing in a city where no one knew me, and was accepted in Manitoba at the hospital where I'd been born before my father was transferred to Saskatchewan. A month before my eighteenth birthday, I arrived back at Misericordia, the hospital I'd left when I was five days old. There, I slept on a cot in a room I shared with two strangers. We each had a locker similar to the ones in high school and were expected to store all our belongings in it. The bathroom in the hall had no lock and was shared by all the girls on our second floor.

In two weeks I came to hear the word "misery" whenever anyone said the word Misericordia. In the late fifties, nursing students worked the wards immediately after their arrival, changing beds and bathing patients. I had no brothers and had never seen my parents or sisters naked. I ran away the morning I was scheduled to bathe a man, and returned to be reprimanded when darkness fell and I had nowhere else to go. The next day I was put on the terminal ward to bathe an old woman. She whimpered when I touched her with my soapy cloth. I promised

only three ages for women in Hollywood – Babe, District Attorney,

myself that I would not allow a stranger to bathe my grandma when she was dying.

On secret ballots, the girls in my class voted me their Freshie Queen. I was expected to compete with other girls from other careers for the crown awarded to the most beautiful student. I woke up from nightmares of bright lights shining on my freckled face. I felt ashamed for pretending to be someone I wasn't. I made an appointment with Mother Superior, the woman none of us had seen. In her dimly lit office, she reminded me that my classmates were depending on me to prove myself a worthy candidate. I phoned home to ask my mother why she had given birth in a Catholic hospital when we were Presbyterians. She said she trusted nuns not to think about their boyfriends while she was in labor, and remained deaf to my plea to return home.

In spite of her, I got on a train for the twelve-hour ride back to Saskatchewan. My father and grandmother stood on the platform, their arms open to welcome me. Mother's absence was her way of saying she was ashamed of me. I steeled myself against her attempts to make me right my wrong by returning to the hospital.

Years later, living alone on my thirtieth birthday, I enrolled at university to finish the degree I'd been laboring over at night classes for years while I spent my daylight hours as a secretary. In autumn, I moved to Vancouver and at age thirty-five graduated with a Master's degree from the University of British Columbia. When I was given a sessional position at the university, my mother expressed her pride in my accomplishment. Just as my heart began to swell, she asked if I'd ever believed I'd graduate and teach at a big university with spectacular rose gardens. Her face crumpled when I told her my achievement had become possible only after I'd escaped her disappointment.

Now, having reached my sixty-sixth birthday and retired from my career, I realize that only in the end do we see the beginning with clarity. Cancer has taken the lives of both my mother and sister. Later, I survived my own cancer and comforted my husband through his. I have seen what a difference devoted nurses make to our well-being. Still, I have not forgotten the disappointment on my mother's face when I came home. Nor have I forgiven myself for the harsh words I used to defend my decision.

As age spots multiply on the backs of my hands, I've come to realize we understand the workings of a mother's heart only after we mature. My mother had grown up on a Canadian homestead where medical help was too far away to contemplate. Now, I take flowers to her grave and whisper how grateful I am that she was finally proud of me. I have learned that affection within families surpasses understanding. I am reminded that I'm beautiful in the only way I can be — in the eyes of those who love themselves enough to love me too. Perhaps our sole responsibility to parents is to be grateful they blessed us with life in all its imperfections.

Vocations Club

Paula Sergi

We met on Tuesdays, after school
with Sister Mary Agnes,
the two Mary Lous, Julie, Kay and me
to learn about being nuns.

harder to have heroes, but it is sort of necessary." Ernest Hemingway

The convent sounded good to me —
a room of my own, a single bed,
time to think and pray, no arguments
over what we'd watch – *Bonanza* versus *Dragnet,*
or who would get the couch.
I dug those crazy nun outfits, and hated hand-me-downs
with too-long sleeves and too-tight waists.
I'd take the smell of polished wood and incense
over burnt grilled cheese and sour milk.
I'd have a good job, teaching kids
and all the chalk I'd want,
long, unbroken pieces that echoed off the board,
all eyes on me as I'd tap directions,
conducting my classroom all day.
People, I'd begin, today we're talking about. . .
whatever I want to!
Nuns got great rosaries with fancy beads
and lots of gifts at Christmas.
And the solitude of celibacy sounded pretty good,
better than worrying about French kissing
like my sister, better than pining for men,
like Mom, whose men left anyway.

Peek-a-Boo Freckles
Linda O'Connell

Freckles, did you slide through my wrinkles and splatter in a
    splotch on my hand?
Please, please, help me understand.

When I was young, I pancake-make-uped you away,
but I wouldn't dare apply that stuff to my face today.

Facial sludge makes wrinkles more pronounced
and so, heavy makeup I've denounced.

I smear slippery night-time cream onto my face and hands
as though I am greasing crevices of crinkled Bundt cake pans.

I wonder freckles, yes I do,
how on earth did you squeeze through?

I tug my face upwards at either side–
Oh, that's where the rest of you freckles hide!

'As She Ages

Kerin Riley-Bishop

Her skin is slightly weathered now
leathered now
I do not know when she got older
I still see myself so young.

It is odd how time passes
how age skips one while settling on another
like a fickle tornado – this house, this house
skip this one.

When lines show on my face
I consider them treasures
trophies of laughter and tears
My years
accumulated; good and bad.

Her skin is weathered now
leathered now
I do not ponder long on how
but, when?

Hold That Thought

Gail Denham

There's a moment.
It includes laughter.
A dance anoints the time
into a sponge that bounces
and jiggles until tears of mirth
make the occasion so juicy,
it nearly slips away, but we
clutch the event hard, close
to our hearts, as if it were
the keys to eternity,

which, of course, it is.

...To Wrinkles

Steve Cartwright

About the Authors

Carol Ayer was born in Berkeley, California, in the early 1960s. She grew up in Orinda, California, and graduated from UC Berkeley. Her publication credits include *Woman's World* magazine, two Chicken Soup series books, *The Prairie Times, The Christian Science Monitor*, and *flashquake*. She has won awards from WOW-Women on Writing, *Artella Magazine*, and *Brady Magazine*.

Roy A. Barnes writes from southeastern Wyoming. His poetry and prose have appeared at *The Goblin Reader, Swimming Kangaroo, Heritage Writer, C/Oasis, Literary Liftoff, Poesia, The First Line,* and *Skive Magazine*. Roy's favorite baseball player is Hall of Famer Reggie Jackson, and his favorite team has always been the New York Yankees.

Glenda Beall reinvented herself in her late fifties, and followed her life-long passion. From writing as a child sitting high in a chinaberry tree, she came full circle and began publishing her work in 1995. She presently serves as Program Coordinator for the North Carolina Writers' Network West. Glenda is on faculty at the John C. Campbell Folk School. She also teaches at a junior college and in a church adult education program. Her classes are for senior adults who want to write about their lives for their children and grandchildren. She is a multi-genre writer, having published poetry in literary magazines, essays in anthologies and slick magazines. One of her stories will appear in *Cup of Comfort for Horse Lovers*. In her "spare" time, Glenda writes articles for the Valley River Humane Society

a stock that would triple its value every year. I told him, at my age, I

newsletter and for local newspapers. She also maintains a blog for her writers' group: www.netwestwriters.blogspot.com.

Betty Wilson Beamguard writes full-time, specializing in magazine features, short fiction, and humorous essays. She has received over 30 honors for her writing, and her work has appeared in *Women in the Outdoors, South Carolina, Sasee, ByLine, The Writer* and more. In her humorous novel, *Weej and Johnnie Hit Florida*, two middle-age women spend a week in Florida trying to lose the jerk who is following them. Her most recent book is the biography of a woman who drives a draft horse with her feet – *How Many Angels Does It Take: The Remarkable Life of Heather Rose Brooks.* www.home.earthlink.net/~bbeamguard.

Renie Burghardt, who was born in Hungary, is a freelance writer with many credits. Her writing has appeared in 60 anthologies, like the Chicken Soup series, *Chocolate for Women,* Cup of Comfort series, Guideposts books, *God Allows U-Turns,* God's Way books, and many others. She has also been published in magazines like *Mature Living, Mature Years, Midwest Living, Missouri Life, Cat Fancy, Angels on Earth,* and others. She lives in a beautiful rural area and loves nature, animals, reading, writing, hiking, gardening, nature photography, and spending time with her friends and family, especially her three granddaughters. You can visit her blog here: www.renieburghardtsworld.blogspot.com.

brenda wise byrd is a grandmother who still lives in the Alabama town where she was born. She began journaling as a young teen and her joy in writing developed from that early beginning. Widowed at 26, she has seen life from a perspective none of us would choose, but one that has given her a greater appreciation of life and everyday pleasures. Much of her writing comes from observing the people and nature around her and transforming those "snapshots" into life lessons and inspirational moments. She has been locally published and is now seeking a broader audience.

Steve Cartwright is a cartoonist, illustrator, writer, and is kind to dogs. He works out of Atlanta and his art has appeared in several magazines, newspapers, books, various websites for commercial and governmental clients, and scribbling – but mostly drooling – on tavern napkins. He creates art *pro bono* for several animal rescue groups and was awarded the 2004 James Award for his cover art for *Champagne Shivers*. The *Cimarron Review* and *Stories for Children* covers display his illustrations. See his website www.angelfire.com/sc2/cartoonsbycartwright where no pixels were injured during the production.

Al Carty is a Californian retired to the high plains of New Mexico. He grows garlic and chilis and roams the piñon-juniper hills and writes about the thoughts he finds there. He has been romancing the Muse for a long time. Sometimes she dances for him and sometimes she hides among his thoughts. Since he discovered that rewriting makes her smile, his stories and poems have been accepted by *Menda City Review, 5th Story Review, Written Word, Anthology Builder, Sage of Consciousness,* and *Cause and Effect Magazine.*

Sally Clark lives in Fredericksburg, Texas, with her husband, their children, and their grandchildren. Sally has practiced for retirement her entire life. When she finally achieved her goal in 2001, Sally began writing stories and poetry for children and adults. Her work has been published in the Chicken Soup series, the Cup of Comfort series, and several of June Cotner's gift books. Her poetry for children appears in Blooming Tree Press' *Summer Shorts* and *Sweet Dreams*. In the Christian field, Howard Books, Integrity Publishers, and Tyndale House have published her stories and poems.

SuzAnne C. Cole writes from a studio in the woods in the Texas Hill Country. She's published more than 350 poems, essays, short stories and articles in commercial and literary magazines, anthologies, and newspapers. She's been both a juried and featured poet at the Houston Poetry Fest and once won a haiku festival in Japan.

---

and forget your age." Norman Vincent Peale ~§~ "My generation,

TJ Coles was raised and lived most of his life in the Pacific Northwest, in a large town that preferred to think of itself as a small town. He spent most of his summers on his grandmother's ranch and has worked as a logger, in mining, as a forest fire fighter, and as a security guard. TJ has been telling stories since he was eight years old. Some of them have even been true. A number of magazines and dozens of online publications have published Coles' work. His day job is in civil engineering.

Ginger B. Collins' sailing tales have appeared in *Cruising World* and *Living Aboard Magazine*. Both *The Atlanta Journal Constitution* and *The Cincinnati Inquirer* have published her articles in their Sunday Travel Sections. She has two pieces of short fiction scheduled this summer in *Pig Iron Press*, a flash fiction story this winter in *LunchHour Stories*, and a story in *Voices of...* anthology, coming early in 2009 from LaChance Publishing. Recently retired from Atlanta to Canada's Cape Breton Island, Ginger and husband, Melvin, plan a retirement of sailing local and distant shorelines. Her web site is www.GingerBCollins.com.

R. Scott Comegys lives in Shreveport, Louisiana, where she is a late-bloomer Boomer. Vintage 1952, she is a single mom with one daughter in college and a son in high school. She toils by day as a civil servant, fondly recollecting manual typewriters with tri-carbon inserts. And, although life is good with digital cable, she dearly misses the Indian Head TV test pattern.

Carole Creekmore, a Baby Boomer who grew up in rural eastern North Carolina, is a widow with two adult children, two lovely granddaughters, and an English bulldog, Okie. With degrees in English from Wake Forest University, she teaches composition, literature, creative writing, and humanities at an Atlanta area college, writes prose and poetry whenever inspired, and enjoys traveling, genealogy, and photography. She has had several articles and poems published over the years, as well as the essay "Holiday Expectations – Then and Now" recently published in *Silver Boomers*.

faced as it grew with a choice between religious belief and existential

Barbara Crooker has been writing poetry for more than 30 years, with credits in magazines such as *The Christian Science Monitor, Margie, Poetry East, Smartish Pace, Nimrod, River City, Yankee, The Beloit Poetry Journal, Poetry International, The Denver Quarterly, America, Highlights for Children,* and anthologies such as *Good Poems For Hard Times* (Viking, edited by Garrison kellion), *Sweeping Beauty: Contemporary Women Poets Do Housework* (University of Iowa Press), and *Boomer Girls* (University of Iowa Press). She has two full-length books, *Radiance* and *Line Dance*, both from Word Press. She grew up in the mid-Hudson Valley in the fifties, went to college in New Jersey in the sixties, and now lives and writes in rural northeastern Pennsylvania.

Barbara Darnall, the daughter of a high school English teacher and a West Texas lawyer and rancher, has been surrounded by words all her life and grew up telling stories and writing scripts for her playmates to perform. She graduated from Baylor University with B.A. and M.A. degrees in drama, and taught at the college level for several years. She writes poetry, articles, and personal narratives, and has written and directed numerous short dramas for her church. She has copyedited one book and several manuscripts, and, as a tax consultant for more than thirty years, she particularly enjoys the letter-writing contests she occasionally gets into with the IRS!

Mary Deal, a native of Walnut Grove, California (in the Sacramento River Delta) has lived in England, the Caribbean, and now resides in Kapaa, Hawaii. She has published three novels: *The Tropics: Child of a Storm – Caught in a Rip – Hurricane Secret*, an adventure trilogy; *The Ka*, a paranormal Egyptian fantasy; and *River Bones*, her first thriller which is set in her childhood hometown area. *Down to the Needle* will be her next thriller due out early 2010 and set along the California coastline. Learn more about Mary, read short stories, novel excerpts, and writing tips on her web site: www.writeanygenre.com.

Gail Denham, a native Oregonian, has showcased her state with poetry, short stories, and photography for over 30 years. Her work has been published in national and international magazines. In addition, she enjoys leading writing workshops. Married, with four sons and (almost) 13 grandchildren, plus two great-grands, she and her husband now live in central Oregon where Denham was raised. Life was quieter and slower when Denham grew up in Redmond and even in the years they brought up their family. She definitely appreciates the simple life best.

Terri Kirby Erickson of Lewisville, North Carolina, is the author of a book of poetry entitled, *Thread Count.* Her work has been published or accepted by *The Broad River Review, The Dead Mule, Pisgah Review, The Christian Science Monitor, Paris Voice, Old Mountain Press, Thieves Jargon, Forsyth Woman,* and the Hickory Women's Resource Center anthology *Voices and Vision: A Collection of Writings By and About Empowered Women.* The Northwest Cultural Council also selected her work in 2006 and 2007 for an international juried poetry exhibit.

Joanne Faries, originally from the Philadelphia area, lives in Texas with her husband Ray. She considers herself fortunate to be able to pursue a writing career after eons in the business world. Published previously in *Doorknobs & Bodypaint,* Joanne writes short stories, flash fiction, and poetry. She has works on ALongStory Short.com, Associatedcontent.com, in *Shine* magazine, *Chicken Soup for the Soul – Kids in the Kitchen,* and has started a novel. Joanne enjoys reading and movies, and is the film critic for the *Little Paper of San Saba.* She is a member of Trinity Writer's Workshop in Bedford, Texas.

Margaret Fieland, born and raised in New York City, has been around art and music all her life. Her poems, articles and children's stories have appeared in, among others, *Main Channel Voices, Echolocation,* and *Stories for Children Magazine.* You may visit her web site, www.margaretfieland.com.

Betty Jo Goddard traveled a packed road since her birth in Windsor, Illinois. While on that road, she acquired a BS from Illinois State, an MA from University of Colorado, and twenty-five years of teaching's bruises, successes, smiles, and love. Betty Jo retired from teaching in 1983, and now lives on a ridge top in Alaska with her three errant huskies. Since retiring from teaching, she's taken up writing as a hobby. This hobby gives her fun, and, when she tosses her lines in the publishing world's waters, enough bites to keep her dogs well fed.

Ginny Greene likely arrived on Planet Earth with a bluepencil clutched in her fist. Past president of Abilene Writers Guild, her writing life includes years of newspaper lifestyle features, a newspaper column, and a handful of newsletters, including seven years editing the Guild's newsletter. For fun, Ginny writes poems and works crossword puzzles. She edits everything, even street signage, especially yard sale signs, even in her sleep. She's happiest seeing her love of words spilled over to her children and grandchildren, including daughter, Karen, also a Silver Boomer Books editor. While still loving her Northwest hometown, Ginny is at home with Larry near Abilene, Texas, and her grown family. Ginny's book *Song of County Roads* is scheduled for publication in the fall of 2008.

Rhoda Greenstone, for the past two decades, has instructed Southern California college students in the joys of language arts and humanities. In a former life, she served as editor, feature writer, critic, and photo-journalist for many publications, including *The Hollywood Reporter*, *Los Angeles Times*, *Malibu Times*, and *Classics West Magazine*. A chapter she wrote deconstructing her poem "A Letter From L.A." will appear in *Poem, Revised* (Marion Street Press) in 2008. Her poetry, short stories and essays have appeared in various journals. Currently she is arbitrating with a muse who insists on dictating – at the least convenient times – a novel about a family of artists set to self destruct, called *Lost Paradise*.

Becky Haigler is retired after 24 years of teaching Spanish and reading in Texas public secondary schools. Her poetry has appeared in national and regional periodicals. Her short stories for adolescents have been published by several denominational publishing houses. Two of her magic realism stories are included in the anthology *Able to...* (NeoNuma Arts Press, 2006.) Becky currently resides in Shreveport, Louisiana, with her husband Dave Haigler. She is the mother of two daughters and grandmother of three granddaughters. Becky is currently working on a collection of magic realism stories. More of her poetry appears on her family blog, www.xanga.com/anchorpoet.

Heather Haldeman, who lives in Pasadena, California, began writing nine years ago after her oldest son left for college. She has been married to her husband, Hank, for 29 years and has three children. She has published several personal essays and is currently writing a book.

Joy Harold Helsing is an ex-salesclerk, ex-secretary, ex-textbook editor, ex-psychologist, ex-college instructor, ex-New Englander, ex-San Franciscan who now lives in the Sierra Nevada foothills of Northern California. Her work has appeared in *Bellowing Ark, Brevities, Byline, California Quarterly, Centrifugal Eye, Leading Edge, The Mid-America Poetry Review, Möbius, Poetalk, Poetry Depth Quarterly, The Raintown Review, Rattlesnake Review, Writers' Journal,* and elsewhere. She has published three chapbooks and one book, *Confessions of the Hare* (PWJ Publishing).

Frances Hern splits her time between Calgary, Alberta, and Golden, British Columbia, both in Canada, where she writes poetry, non-fiction and children's fiction. Her books include *Norman Bethune* (James Lorimer), *Arctic Explorers* (Heritage House) and *Aunt Maud's Mittens* (Scholastic Canada). She has also recently published poetry and prose in *Silver Boomers* and *Poetry for Big Kids* (Neil Harding McAlister).

La Rochefoucauld ~§~ *"My only fear is that I may live too long. This*

Linda Oatman High is the author of 21 books, as well as a journalist/poet/songwriter. Linda's newest book is *The Hip Grandma's Handbook*, and Linda blogs regularly on www.hipgrandma.com, a site for (cool) Boomer grandmothers. Earning her MFA at Vermont College, she will graduate the same year that her grandson graduates from kindergarten! A frequent presenter at conferences, libraries, and schools, Linda may be contacted at lohigh@frontiernet.net.

Jeanne Holtzman is an aging hippie, writer and women's health care practitioner, not necessarily in that order. Born in the Bronx, she prolonged her adolescence as long as possible in Vermont and currently lives with her husband and daughter in Massachusetts. Her writing has appeared or is forthcoming in such publications as *The Providence Journal, Writer's Digest, The First Line, Twilight Times, Chick Flicks, flashquake, Salome, Hobart Pulp online, Hip Mama, EveryDay Fiction* and *The Iconoclast*. You may reach Jeanne at J.holtzman@comcast.net.

Jo Anne Horn is a self-proclaimed dabbler. She dabbles in writing, oil painting, playing piano and says she has just enough talent to keep herself amused. She worked as a secretary in various fields before remarrying in 1975. She attended The University of Texas at San Antonio for two years before relocating to Lake Brownwood, Texas. For twelve years, she worked, along with her husband, as an EMT with their volunteer fire department.

Juleigh Howard-Hobson's work has recently appeared in *Lucid Rhythms, The Barefoot Muse, Mezzo Cammin, Umbrella, The Chimaera, Loch Raven Review, Every Day Stories, Shatter Colors Literary Review, The Raintown Review, Mobius, Fourteen Magazine, Perspectives* and...*Silver Boomers*. She is a tail-end member of the Baby Boom generation, a bit more punk rock than Woodstock.

Michael Lee Johnson, a poet and freelance writer, is self-employed in advertising and selling custom promotional products. He's author of *The Lost American: From Exile to Freedom*, has published two chapbooks of poetry, is nominated for the James B. Baker Award in poetry (Sam's Dot Publishing), and contributed poetry to *Silver Boomers*. Currently living in Itasca, Illinois, U.S.A., he lived in Canada during the Vietnam era and will be published (early 2008) in the anthology *Crossing Lines: Poets Who Came to Canada in the Vietnam War Era*. His web sites include poetryman.mysite.com where his other sites are linked.

Karen Karlitz grew up in Forest Hills, New York, during the 1960s. (What she remembers, she thoroughly enjoyed.) She worked as an associate editor and writer for *Pharmacy Times* magazine before relocating to California. For several years she was a regular contributor to the *Los Angeles Times*, and also worked as a writer and editor for *Beverly Hills 90210* and the *Brentwood News*, and *Santa Monica Sun*. Her work has appeared in these publications, as well as in the *Miranda Literary Magazine* and the *Foliate Oak Literary Magazine*. Currently, she lives and writes short stories in south Florida.

James Keane resides in northern New Jersey with his wife and son and a menagerie of merry pets. He has been writing and revising his poetry over the course of the hundred years since he earned bachelor's and master's degrees in English Literature at Georgetown University. He has been privileged to have his poems appear, most recently, in *The Houston Literary Review*, *Tipton Poetry Journal*, *The Chimaera*, *Taj Mahal Review*, and *Contemporary American Voices*, where he was the Featured Poet of the August 2007 issue.

Helga Kidder has lived in the Tennessee hills for 30 years, raised two daughters, half a dozen cats, and a few dogs. She received her BA in English from the University of Tennessee, and MFA in Writing from Vermont College. She is co-founder of the

Chattanooga Writers Guild and leads their poetry group. Her poetry and translations have appeared in *The Louisville Review, The Southern Indiana Review, The Spoon River Poetry Review, Comstock Review, Eleventh Muse, Snake Nation Review, Voices International, Moebius, Free Focus, Phoenix, Chug,* and others, and three anthologies.

Blanche L. Ledford is a native of Hayesville, North Carolina. She grew up during the Great Depression in the Blue Ridge Mountains of western North Carolina and often writes about that time. Her work has appeared in *Blue Ridge Guide; Lights in the Mountains; Looking Back; Sand, Sea & Sail; Night Whispers*; and other journals. She's an avid reader and member of Georgia Mountain Writer's Club.

Brenda Kay Ledford is a native of Hayesville, North Carolina. Her work has appeared in *Pembroke Magazine, Asheville Poetry Review, Appalachian Heritage*, and other journals. She is listed with *A Directory of American Poets and Fiction Writers*. Ledford received the 2007 Paul Green Multimedia Award from North Carolina Society of Historians for her poetry chapbook, *Shew Bird Mountain*. Her poetry book, *Sacred Fire*, is upcoming with Finishing Line Press. She is a member of North Carolina Writers' Network, North Carolina Poetry Society and Georgia Poetry Society. For more information go to her website: www.brendakayledford.com.

Larry Lefkowitz' stories, poems, and humor have been published in literary reviews and magazines in the U.S., England, and Israel where he lives. He has self-published humor books, and is currently trying to find a publisher for his novel *Lieberman*. It concerns the assistant to a literary critic who is asked by the critic's wife following her husband's death to complete his unfinished novel. Though set in Israel, the novel is universal in theme and is replete with literary allusions. Larry is also trying to find a publisher for his detective novel, *Trouble in Jades* about a series of murders in a jades museum.

Rose F. Kennedy ~§~ "The quality, not the longevity, of one's life is

Denton Loving makes his home in Speedwell, Tennessee. He works in the advancement offices at Lincoln Memorial University, where he also assists directing the Mountain Heritage Literary Festival. His short story, "Authentically Weathered Lumber," was chosen in 2007 as the first winner of the Gurney Norman Prize for Short Fiction, a contest judged by Mr. Norman through the literary journal *Kudzu*. Loving's poetry has also appeared in *The Birmingham Arts Journal.*

Eileen Malone lives in the coastal fog of the San Francisco Bay Area where she directs the Soul-Making Literary Competition, which she founded in 1994, and hosts/produces "Pen Women Presents," interviews with creative people on Access San Francisco Channel 29. She is widely published, and last year two of her poems were nominated for Pushcart prizes.

Arlene Mason is an author and freelance technical writer who lives with her husband, a miniature poodle and a calico cat outside Dallas, Texas. She writes on a variety of topics, drawing from her diverse experience. She has contributed articles to a varied collection of online and print magazines. She says that writing keeps her sane; most people agree.

Janet McCann has poetry in journals such as *Kansas Quarterly, Parnassus, Nimrod, Sou'wester, Christian Century, Christianity and Literature, New York Quarterly, Tendril, Poetry Australia,* and *McCall's,* among many others.

Lyn Messersmith is a third generation rancher, a freelance writer, newspaper columnist, and purveyor of horse sense, nonsense, and occasional wisdom. She is affiliated with Nebraska and South Dakota Humanities Councils and, with a friend, offers writing workshops and historical programs of original music and poetry based on the lives of people who helped open the West.

Lyn has published two books of poetry. *Ground Tied* won a 2004 Will Rogers Medallion Award from the Academy of Western Artists.

Her book of daily reflections is titled *My Sister Mariah; the Journal of a Windwalker.*

Anthony J. Mohr writes from his home in southern California. His essays, memoirs, and short stories have appeared in *Bibliophilos, The Christian Science Monitor, Circle Magazine, Currents, Literary House Review, The Sacramento Bee, Skyline Magazine,* and *Word Riot.* Two of his works have been nominated for the Pushcart Prize. His hobbies include hiking, travel, horseback riding, and improv theater.

Michael Neal Morris has published online and in print in *Borderlands, Lynx Eye, The Concho River Review, Illya's Honey, The Distillery, Dogwood Tales Magazine, The GW Review, Liberty Hill Poetry Review, The Mid-South Review, Chronogram, Contemporary Rhyme, Haruah, T-Zone, Flash-Flooding, Glassfire Magazine,* and *Mouth Full of Bullets.* He lives with his wife and children just outside Dallas, and teaches at Eastfield College. He is seeking publication of his first collection of stories, *The End of the Argument,* and his collection of poems, *Wrestling Light.*

Sheryl L. Nelms, Kansas native, graduated from South Dakota State University in Family Relations and Child Development. Her poems, stories and articles have appeared in periodicals and anthologies including *Readers' Digest, Modern Maturity, Capper's, Kaleidoscope, Grit, Cricket,* over 4,500 times. Twelve collections of her poetry have been published.

Sheryl has taught writing and poetry at conferences, colleges and schools. She was a Bread Loaf Contributor at the Bread Loaf Writer's Conference, Middlebury, Vermont. She has served as editor for many journals, including her current post as essay editor of *The Pen Woman Magazine,* the membership magazine of the National League of American Pen Women. She holds membership in The Society of Southwestern Authors, Abilene Writers Guild, and Trinity Arts Writers Association.

thought, that when Mozart was my age he had been dead for two

Karen Neuberg is retired after 40 years working as an information specialist, public librarian, marketing researcher, and social worker. Her work has appeared or is pending in literary journals and anthologies including *Phoebe, Poems Niederngasse, 42Opus, Louisville Review,* and *Riverine, An Anthology of Hudson Valley Writers.* She's a Pushcart and Best of the Net nominee, holds an MFA from the New School, and lives in Brooklyn and West Hurley, New York, with her husband. They are about to become grandparents for the second time.

Linda O'Connell's work has appeared in several Chicken Soup series books, numerous anthologies, periodicals and literary magazines. Linda is a seasoned early-childhood teacher in St. Louis, Missouri. She also teaches a senior citizen memoir writing class. She and her husband, Bill, have a blended family of four adult children, and nine grandchidren who tickle their fancy.

Quanah Parker, Kansas-born in 1946, is a distant cousin of his Comanche Chief namesake. His family moved to Abilene, Texas, then Norman, Oklahoma, returning to Abilene so Quanah and older brother Quay could attend Abilene Christian University, "getting them away from Philistine OU women." Both brothers sold Bibles to put themselves through college and law school. After University of Texas Law, Lt. Parker led an Army MP Platoon from 1971 to 1972 and was a Captain in the Reserves from 1974 to 1982. An Abilene resident, he's practiced law for 35 years. His daughter Padgett and son Paden live in Austin, and son, Pride, daughter-in-law Allison, and granddaughter Pressley in Houston.

Meg Pearce lives in northern Ontario with her retired military firefighter husband and is surrounded by most of her family. Some of her short stories can be found in the anthology *Confabulation* published by Winterblue Publishing in June, 2008.

Yvonne Pearson is a writer and clinical social worker who lives in Minneapolis, Minnesota. Her poetry and essays have appeared in a variety of publications, including *Sing, Heavenly Muse!, Transformations, Wolf Head Quarterly, Poetry Calendar 2000*, and *Studio One*. She is the recipient of a Loft Creative Non-Fiction Award, has participated in readings at The Loft, the University of Minnesota, and the American Association of University Women, St. Paul branch, and is the co-author of several books.

James Penha, a native New Yorker, has lived for the past sixteen years in Indonesia. *No Bones to Carry*, Penha's most recent volume of poetry, is available from New Sins Press at www.newsinspress.com. Among the most recent of his many other published works are articles in the *NCTE's Classroom Notes Plus*; fiction at *East of the Web, BigPulp,* and *Ignavia*; and poems in *THEMA* and in the anthologies *Queer Collection* (Fabulist Flash Publishing), *Only the Sea Keeps: Poetry of the Tsunami* (Bayeux Press), and *Silver Boomers*. Penha edits a web site for current-events poetry at www.newversenews.com.

Diana M. Raab, M.F.A., essayist, memoirist and poet, teaches at the UCLA Extension Writers' Program and the Santa Barbara Writers Conference. A columnist for InkByte.com, she writes and lectures on journaling. Her memoir *Regina's Closet: Finding My Grandmother's Secret Journal* is a finalist for Best Book of the Year by *ForeWord Magazine*. She has two poetry collections, *My Muse Undresses Me* and *Dear Anais: My Life in Poems for You*. Her writing has appeared in *The Writer, Writers Journal, Skylight Review, Rosebud, The Louisville Review, Palo Alto Review, Oracle, The Binnacle, Homestead,* and *Red River Review*. She's the recipient of the Benjamin Franklin Book Award for *Getting Pregnant and Staying Pregnant: Overcoming Infertility and High Risk Pregnancy*. Visit her web site: www.dianaraab.com.

Kerin Riley-Bishop is an editor and partner of Silver Boomer Books. She is a poet, photographer and casual painter. A deep spirituality and love of nature provide ample fuel for her writing endeavors. She is a member of local writing and critique

to live long enough." Groucho Marx ~§~ *"The older I grow the more*

groups, and currently has several writing and photography projects pending. She lives in West Texas with her partner, Mason, and their two children.

Barbara B. Rollins lives in Abilene, Texas, a judge who writes while waiting for lawyers. A member of SCBWI, her children's books include the novel *Syncopated Summer* and a forensic series *Fingerprint Evidence, Ballistics, Cause of Death,* and *Blood Evidence.* Her work has appeared in *Byline, Kidz Ch@t, R*A*D*A*R,* and *Off the Record, an anthology of poetry by lawyers.* The past president of Abilene Writers Guild maintains the group's web site as well as those of other nonprofit organizations besides her www.SharpWriters.com. Like many Baby Boomers, she shares her husband with two dogs while worrying about aging parents, two sons, and daughters-in-law. She is a principal in Silver Boomer Books.

Doug Sellers, a lifetime manic-depressive, encourages others dealing with the condition. Now age 77, he retired from school teaching in 1979. He lives simply and writes about good times from his past. He keeps membership in Abilene Writers Guild current (1992 to present), and wins awards in their contests. Doug lives with his wife of 37 years, Ruth, on a farm in Runnels County where he stores his collection of antique farm machinery. He graduated from Hardin-Simmons University, 1970, with a Master's Degree in Administrative Education. He is a veteran of the U.S. Air Force, 1952 to 1956.

Ruth Sellers, 83 years old and a retired teacher, lives with her husband, Doug, on a farm in Runnels County, Texas. She has written for publication since the early 1990s. Her credits include *Crafts 'n' Things, World and I, History Magazine,* newspaper articles in *Abilene Reporter-News, Winters Enterprise, Ballinger Ledger,* and prizes in many writers' contests. She taught school at primary level and at the Reading Center in Abilene, Texas. She has done freelance writing since her retirement from teaching in 1980, and is a past president of Abilene Writers Guild.

"I distrust the familiar doctrine that age brings wisdom." H. L.

Paula Sergi is the author of *Family Business*, a collection of poems from Finishing Line Press, May, 2005, and co-editor of *Boomer Girls: Poems by Women from the Baby Boom Generation*, University of Iowa Press, 1999. She received a Wisconsin Arts Board Artist Fellowship in 2001. Her poetry is published regularly in such journals as *The Bellevue Literary Review, Primavera, Crab Orchard Review, Spoon River Poetry Review* and *The American Journal of Nursing*. She holds an MFA in creative writing from Vermont College and a BSN from the University of Wisconsin, Madison.

Elizabeth Simpson was a college instructor and continues to run an Author-Reading Series. She has published two nonfiction books: *The Perfection of Hope: Journey Back to Health* (1997), nominated for the B.C.Book Prize and VanCity Award and translated into Spanish; and *One Man at a Time: Confessions of a Serial Monogomist* (2000), nominated for the B.C.Book Prize. She has also published short stories: *Slipping the Noose* (Seal Press 2004). Two of her short stories were broadcast on CBC radio: "Dressed for Suicide" (April 2002) and "Puppy Love" (October 2003). Currently she is working on a novel, *The Marmalade Moon*.

J. J. Steinfeld, fiction writer, poet, and playwright, lives in Charlottetown, Prince Edward Island, Canada. He has published a novel, *Our Hero in the Cradle of Confederation* (Pottersfield Press), nine short story collections, three by Gaspereau Press – *Should the Word Hell Be Capitalized?, Anton Chekhov Was Never in Charlottetown,* and *Would You Hide Me?* – and a poetry collection, *An Affection for Precipices* (Serengeti Press). His short stories and poems have appeared in numerous anthologies and periodicals internationally, and over thirty of his one-act and full-length plays have been performed in Canada and the United States.

Judith Strasser has published two poetry collections, *Sand Island Succession: Poems of the Apostle*s and *The Reason/Unreason Project*, and a memoir, *Black Eye: Escaping a*

Marriage, Writing a Life. Her work has appeared widely in literary journals, including *Poetry, The Kenyon Review, Witness,* and *Prairie Schooner.* Her blog, In Lieu of Speech, reflects on her life as a survivor of metastatic stomach cancer. (www.inlieuofspeech.blogspot.com)

Kathie Sutherland is a Canadian poet, essayist and workshop facilitator. Her journaling workshops promote awareness and personal growth, and empower others to find meaning and purpose in their everyday experiences. She is passionate about journaling for self-discovery. Her prose was recently published in *Silver Boomers; Outside of Ordinary: Women's Stories of Transformation; WestWord,* membership magazine of the Alberta Writers Guild; *Canadian Grandparent; The Toronto Globe & Mail;* and *The Edmonton Journal.* Her poetry appears on the following web sites www.women-at-heart.com; www.blueskiespoetry.ca; and www.leafpress.ca.

Andrea Zamarripa Theisen was born and raised in Uvalde, Texas. At age 13, she dropped out of 7th grade to begin working full time. She started writing in her late 40s, contributing to the newspaper *La Voz de Uvalde, Catholic Digest,* and South West Texas Junior College's *The Palm Leaf.*

Lisa Timpf lives near Everett, Ontario, where she enjoys walking in the woods, observing nature, and organic gardening. Her poetry and creative non-fiction have appeared in a variety of venues, including *The Country Connection, Canadian Stories, Creemore Echo,* and *Horizon Magazine.* Her writing credits include one non-fiction book, entitled *St. George's Lawn Tennis Club: The First Hundred Years.*

Suellen Wedmore, Poet Laureate *emerita* for the small seaside town of Rockport, Massachusetts, has been awarded first place in the *Writer's Digest* rhyming poem contest and was selected as an international winner in the *Atlanta Review* annual contest. Recently her chapbook *Deployed* was selected as winner of the Grayson Press chapbook contest and she was selected for a writing residency at Devil's Tower, Wyoming. After 24 years working as a speech and language therapist in the public schools, she retired to enter the MFA Program in Poetry at New England College, graduating in 2004.

Jim Wilson is a veterinarian in private practice for 31 years who seven years ago began treating his poetry seriously and saving it. He now has four published books: *Distillations of a Life Just Lived*, 2002; *Coal to Diamonds*, 2003; *Taking a Peek*, 2004; and *Down to Earth Poetry*, 2006. He's been published recently in *Border Senses*, U.T. El Paso; *Concho River Review*, Angelo State University; *The Desert Candle*, Sul Ross State University; and *Spiky Palm* Texas A&M University at Galveston, and won sweepstakes in the Cisco Writer's Club annual contest for 2007. He says, "I write about everyday events every day."

Thelma Zirkelbach, aka Lorna Michaels, has published thirteen romance novels. Recent widowhood has shifted her focus from romance to personal essay. She enjoys reading, traveling, and spending time with her granddaughter, who also likes to write.

Attributions

Melmac – over 350 manufacturers of melamine dinnerware between 1945 and 1965 ~§~ Necco ® wafers – oldest continuous candy, 8 flavors, by Oliver Chase, English immigrant, Chase & Company first, 1847, then New England Confectionary Co (Necco), went with Arctic expedition in 1913, Adm. Byrd took 2-1/2 tons to South Pole in the '30s ~§~ polyester – 1941 ~§~ Sam I Am – from *Green Eggs & Ham*, Dr. Seuss, 1960 & 1988 ~§~ "Yakity Yak – Don't Talk Back" – Coasters, 1958 ~§~ Sears catalogs – limited catalog begun in 1888 by Richard Sears evolved into varied product catalog starting with 1894 issue ~§~ Crayons – first by Binney & Smith, Crayola, in 1903. Crayon is a color stick for drawing, writing ~§~ Bonomo's Turkish Taffy, by Victor Bonomo (Coney Island candy-making family, with Turkish roots) began as a nickel bar after WWII, not a taffy, but a short nougat, distributed by Woolworth candy counters, bought by Tootsie Roll Industries of Chicago 1980, ceased 1989 ~§~ Orlon ® – acrylic fiber by DuPont, 1941 till 1990 ~§~ Oklahoma dustbowl – 1930-1936, over 100 million acres in Texas Panhandle, Oklahoma, New Mexico, Colorado, Kansas ~§~ Ford's Model A – from October 1927 through 1931, after the Model T ~§~ "Ring of Fire" – Johnny Cash, 1963, Columbia Records ~§~ *Field of Dreams* – released 1989 ~§~ Saran Wrap – polyvinylidene, accidental discovery in 1933 by Ralph Wiley of Dow Chemical, used industrially until it became a food wrap in 1953, now by S.C. Johnson ~§~ *I Love Lucy* – situation comedy 1951-1957, Lucy & Desi Arnaz, Vivian Vance, William Frawley ~§~ Band-Aids ® – Johnson & Johnson, from 1920s, invented by Earle Dickson, produced in New Jersey plant since 1957 ~§~ Chiclets ® – peppermint gum, first by Frank H. Fleer in 1906, then Warner-Lambert, Pfiser, then Cadbury Adams. Fleer joined the 1899 gum manufacturer's merger, American Chicle Co., in 1914. ~§~ Fluoride treatments – 1955 FDA approved stannous fluoride for toothpaste ~§~ Jujubes – candy by German immigrant, Henry Heide, Heide Company, before 1920 ~§~ Junior Mints – 1949 Welch's, now Tootsie Roll Industries ~§~ Goobers ® – from 1925 Blumenthal Chocolate Co., in 1984 Nestlé ~§~ PEZ – 1927, Austrian mint, with the dispenser, PEZ Candy, Inc. ~§~ Sno-Caps ® – a Blumenthal product, from 1920s, now Nestlé ® ~§~ Wax bottles – juice filled, chewable wax ~§~ WD-40 ® – 1953, Rocket Chemical Company began research, settled on the 40th formula, still used today. Used on Atlas Missile first, then appeared on San Diego store shelves 1958. Renamed to WD-40 Company Inc. in 1969 ~§~ Beech Nut Gum – one product of the Beech-Nut Packing Co. ~§~ Woolworth's – Founded by Frank Winfield Woolworth in 1879, popularity declined in 1980s, now only

takes a long time to become young." Pablo Picasso ~§~ *Grandmother*

overseas ~§~ Breck hairspray – Breck shampoo (1930) one of the first liquid shampoos in the U.S., products rebranded in the '70s ~§~ Erace – concealer by Max Factor 1954, Proctor & Gamble Co., 1991 ~§~ box of Keks – German biscuit (cookie) produced by Bahlsen Food Co. since 1891 ~§~ Mackey's Sport Shop – sport and athletic supplier for Abilene, Texas, area from at least the '40s, closed its North 1st and Willis store in the '70s or '80s ~§~ Depends ® – Invented 1980, Bob Beaudrie (The Bear) – Kimberly Clark ~§~ Oreck – founded in 1963 in Cookeville, Tennessee by David Oreck, entrepreneur, age 84 ~§~ Coke ® – soda fountain drink concocted by Dr. John Pemberton, 1886. Coca Cola ® ~§~ Tonka Toys ® – begun in 1947, Minnesota, Hasbro uses 119,000 lbs yellow paint annually ~§~ "Moon River" – Andy Williams, Lyrics by Johnny Mercer, Music Henry Mancini 1961 ~§~ "Tequila" (song) – instrumental by the band Champs 1958 ~§~ Cole Haan shoes – Nike's fashion shoes division, founded 1928 by Trafton Cole and Eddie Haan ~§~ Laundromat – coin operated since 1950s ~§~ Pillsbury Doughboy ® – Poppin Fresh, mascot of Pillsbury Company since 1965 ~§~ The *Brady Bunch* – TV show 1969-1974 ~§~ Hostess ® cupcake – 1919, D.R. "Doc" Rice added seven squiggles and filling 1950 ~§~ *Farmer's Almanac (The Old Farmer's Almanac)* – forecasts determined by a secret formula by founder Robert B. Thomas, since 1792 ~§~ Insert tobacco – Insert Smoking Tobacco, an economic pouch or envelope of loose tobacco that fit into fancy tobacco tins, found now in collectibles and antiques ~§~ Blue Waltz toilet water – popular scent from the '50s ~§~ Flame-Glo lipstick – 1967, later Flame Glow, Del Laboratories, Inc. ~§~ Esther Williams movie – teen swim champ, headed for Olympics until WWII canceled her opportunity, became Hollywood star, swimming in movies, born 8/8/21 in Los Angeles, died 5/25/92 ~§~ Chapstick ® – invented 1880s, now mfg. Wyeth Corporation ~§~ Red Goose shoes – 1869, sold in St. Louis, Missouri, to pioneers moving west, Red Goose Shoes trademarked 1906 ~§~ Ritalin – methylphenidate, synthesized 1944, 1954 patent by Ciba Pharmaceutical Co. ~§~ Cub Scout – officially begun 1930 for younger siblings of Scouts, 20 years after Boy Scouts of America formed in U.S. 1910 ~§~ "Somewhere Over the Rainbow" – Judy Garland, music by Harold Arlen, lyrics by E.Y. Harburg 1939 ~§~ *Bonanza* – Cartwright family spent 14 TV seasons on Ponderosa Ranch 1959-1973. Ben Cartwright and sons Adam, Hoss, Little Joe ~§~ *Pollyanna* – novel by Eleanor H. Porter, 1913 ~§~ Tretinoin – acne treatment ~§~ Miss Clairol – products brought from Europe by chemist Larry Gelb in the Depression years, Miss Clairol created 1950, now Worldwide Beauty Care Group, Proctor & Gamble Co. ~§~ Nutrasweet ® – FDA approved sweetener 1981, NutraSweet Company, now Monsanto ~§~ Aqua Net ® – hairspray, since the '50s, Lornamead ~§~ Shalimar – perfume by Guerlain, 1925 ~§~ "Tennessee Waltz" – by Redd Stewart and PeeWee King 1947, popularized by Patti Page 1950 ~§~ Mr. Coffee – 1972 by North American Systems, Inc., Cleveland, Ohio ~§~ Entenmann's chocolate chips – bakery of German immigrant William Entenmann in NY 1898, best seller chocolate chips since 1974 ~§~ Wiffleball ® – 1953 by Grandfather Mullany, testing found eight oblong perforations work best, no one knows why.

---

to teased child: "I love your freckles. Freckles are beautiful." Child:

Tradition, begun with *Silver Boomers*, bids us reveal our
cyber editing problems, and so here—

I'm Coming Down with Something
the Quartet

Toboggan...
Isn't that a sled?

usage these days is common,
beanie, skullcap, tam, toboggan

so new it's not even in the dictionary
though accepted widely

maybe substitute another word,
a proper dictionary definition

is it regional? a Southern expression?
our book is for a wider market

we could do a starred footnote,
you know – a star and a definition

like this —
* a cap, tam, beanie, skullcap

"Really?" "Of course. Just name one thing prettier than freckles."

Oh. No. Not finished with this —
I can't stop myself, can't let it go yet,
till I spill the silly thought —
* this toboggan's for your noggin'!

What are we going to do with all this candy?!
It IS a trademarked product.
AUGGHH! (Is that how Charlie Brown spells it?)
Maybe AARRGGHH! for ®

The inconsistency in capitals and punctuation
is making me crazy!

What did we do with dates?
Dates? I thought they were plums.
1960's, 1950s, '60's, '70s?
Oh, those dates – lived them large!
Put on your red hat, Mama.

Who voted a five for this piece?
Not me! I'll trade you —
one childhood fantasy
for one teen romance.
Throw in one Alzheimers essay
and it's a deal.

Comma, colon, hyphen, dash,
dingbats, quotes and other hash —
my eyes are crossed, I have a rash —
I'm sure it's Editors' Balderdash.

Child, peering intensely into grandmother's face whispered, "Wrinkles."

Printed in the United States
203832BV00002B/139-525/P